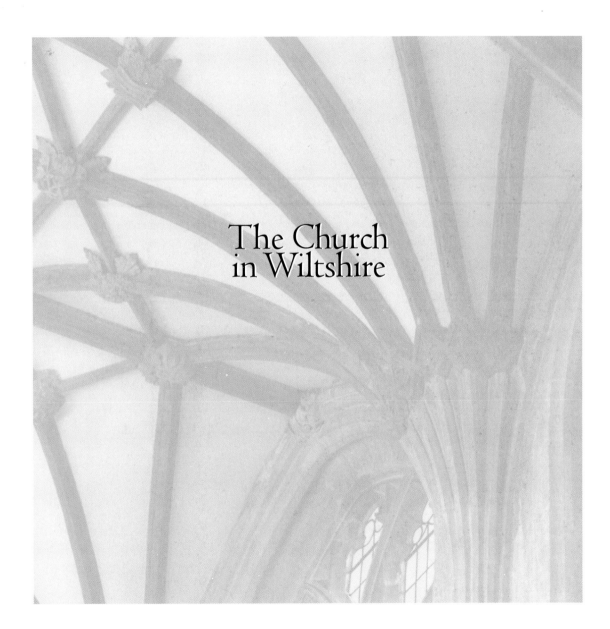

The Church
in Wiltshire

The Church in Wiltshire

text by
John Chandler

photography and gazetteer by
Derek Parker

This is a revised edition of *Wiltshire Churches, an Illustrated History*, first published in 1993 by Alan Sutton Publishing Ltd.

This edition published in the United Kingdom in 2006 by Hobnob Press, PO Box 1838, East Knoyle, Salisbury SP3 6FA

British Library Cataloguing in Publication Data
A catalogue record for this book is available from the British Library.

ISBN 0-946418-46-2

Typeset in 12/16 pt Centaur, and Futura Light
Typesetting and origination by John Chandler
Printed in Great Britain by Salisbury Printing Company Ltd, Salisbury

The frontispiece illustration is a detail from a window by Laurence Whistler in St Peter's Church, Milton Lilbourne. The half-titlepage background is part of a vault in St Mary's Church, Steeple Ashton. The front cover illustration is the Baynton Chapel, Bromham. The back cover illustration is a sculpture of the Virgin and Child in St John Baptist Church, Inglesham.

Contents

Preface to the First Edition

WHY DO PEOPLE visit churches? Some are drawn there to worship, of course, and for them their church or chapel has a spiritual importance outweighing anything architectural or picturesque. For others church visiting is a pleasant hobby – they are the crew, in Philip Larkin's poem, 'that tap and jot and know what rood-lofts were'. But many, perhaps the majority, who take the trouble to find an unlocked door, and whose names are subsequently preserved in the visitors book, seem to have come there simply because church visiting is a part of our national culture, just as the church itself is an essential feature of our English landscape. They are on holiday perhaps, or are spending Sunday afternoon exploring a piece of countryside. The church appeals because it has an atmosphere, a pleasing blend of history and sincerity, craftsmanship and reassurance.

And because we are so used to them, and the way they are dissected for us in the clammy guide, or the dog-eared leaflet, or the faded typescript glued to a 'bat' (for the use of visitors) – because of all this, we are apt to take churches for granted, and not to see them for what they are, the extraordinary survivals of a thousand years or more of human endeavour and tradition.

This is a book for the ordinary church visitor. It is not intended as an academic textbook on church history, nor as a comprehensive survey of religious architecture. What it attempts to do is first, through its illustrations, to show just how rich and diverse a heritage of artistic achievement exists in the churches of a single county; and second, for those who thought that studying them was only a matter of piscinas and lancet windows, to introduce through its text the great farrago of social history, geography, folklore, archaeology and popular culture which is woven into the fabric of even the humblest of our religious buildings.

The prophet Ezekiel has a striking image of a valley full of dry bones, which gradually came together and were articulated, clothed in sinew, flesh and skin; and then the Lord breathed new life into them from the four winds so that they lived again. The aim of this short book is not so exalted, but if we have managed a little sinew, at least, on the bones of Wiltshire's church architecture, we shall be well pleased.

There has been a division of labour in producing this book. The idea for it was Derek Parker's, and he has been responsible for all the photographs, as well as the gazetteer and part of the epilogue. The remainder of the text has been written by John Chandler, and he has also provided the index. But we have each benefited from the other's comments and criticisms.

Derek Parker would like to acknowledge the great assistance given him with the photography by Michael le Masurier; and the many incumbents and others who have given him access to the buildings in their care. John Chandler is most grateful to Michael Marshman and the local studies staff of Wiltshire County Council, Library and Museum Service, for their constructive interpretation of the borrowing regulations; and to Alison Borthwick for her expert help with several areas of the text. He would also like to pay tribute to the published works of the authors listed in the bibliography, especially Richard Morris and Joseph Bettey. We should both like to express our warm appreciation to David Buxton of Alan Sutton Publishing for his patience and encouragement, and to Clare Bishop for her editorial skills. The illustration on page 49 is reproduced by kind permission of the Wiltshire Archaeological and Natural History Society.

Derek Parker, Devizes
John Chandler, East Knoyle
March 1993

Preface to Second Edition

INTEREST in Wiltshire churches continues, and has perhaps grown during the years that our book has been out of print. For this new edition we have made a number of changes. Many more illustrations have been included and the gazetteer and bibliography have been expanded. Minor alterations and corrections have been made to the text and captions. The book has been redesigned to a different page format and reset in a different typeface, enhancing, we hope, the impact of the illustrations and the general 'feel' of the book. We have slightly changed the book's title and the order of our names on the title page. In part this is because *The Church in Wiltshire* was the title originally intended for the work, but also because since our previous edition an entirely different work, unconnected to ours, has been published (*Wiltshire churches: photographic memories*, by David Parker), and we felt that to retain our original title might have caused confusion.

Derek Parker, Devizes
John Chandler, East Knoyle
March 2006

This and three previous pages: The Labours of the Months, depicted on the vault of Salisbury Cathedral Choir. They are replacements painted in 1870s of medallions destroyed in Wyatt's restoration in 1790. The roundels have been placed in order, beginning with January and ending with December.

The effigies of Sir Thomas Gorges, who died in 1610, and his Swedish wife, lying side by side in Salisbury Cathedral.

Christian Origins

SHIVERING towards the midnight communion as Christmas morning approaches, a congregation of overcoated figures mumbles the accustomed carol. Pew-length families, ladies in hats, old friends and new neighbours, the weekly faithful and the once-a-year occasional, the priest in his vestments – we have all made the effort, and turned out for the service. And beyond us and above us, overwhelmed in the half-lit recesses of medieval stone, we glimpse the monuments to our predecessors – the sailor lost at sea, the hero of a forgotten war, the grief of the widowed squire, parish careers proclaimed for ever in expensive Latin or rustic English. Such behaviour, such architecture, such emotions, together pose more than enough questions for this book to explore.

Religious belief itself is a personal matter, of course, and is seldom exposed to the prying historian and archaeologist. But public worship is different, since it requires buildings, and the apparatus of a ritual. The trauma of bereavement, in particular, brings to the surface religious sentiments which are usually suppressed. For our part, as church historians, we can only discover what religious people have left for us to discover; the rest is speculation.

So we cannot begin by identifying the first Christian in Wiltshire. There were Christians in Roman Britain in the third century, and perhaps earlier; and it is possible that the provincial capital of Cirencester, some 5km from the Wiltshire border, had its own bishop by AD 314. But such suggestions need qualifying. Wiltshire as an administrative entity did not then exist, mention of a bishop at this date does not imply a cathedral or a grand religious hierarchy, and the nature of any Christian commitment in our area may have been quite different from that preached in the middle ages or today.

An accumulating body of evidence from Roman Britain suggests that, after Christianity was adopted as the official religion of the empire in AD 312, many of the wealthier and more influential inhabitants incorporated the Christian God alongside all the other deities of classical, celtic and oriental religions. Such an absorption of various religious ideas – known as syncretism – was commonplace in the ancient world. Indeed the dislike and sporadic persecution of Christianity before 312 stemmed in part from the uncompromising and exclusive stance of church leaders regarding other religions.

The meagre catalogue of possibly Christian archaeological finds from Roman Wiltshire tells us only that the new official religion was recognized here, and that some inhabitants seem to have adopted it. How, why, and with what degree of commitment are questions that cannot be answered.

In a quiet Cotswold valley above Castle Combe, where the Fosse Way strikes its course along the north-west edge of Wiltshire, the site of a Roman temple was excavated by archaeologists between 1956 and 1971. Nettleton temple is believed to have been sacred to Apollo, perhaps here syncretized with a celtic god of the nearby stream, which is now called the Broadmead Brook. During the fourth century its octagonal shrine was altered by the building of partition walls, so as to make it cruciform. The new walls were painted with a geometrical design which included saltires, or 'St Andrew' crosses. In one of the cemeteries at the site the excavators located fifteen bodies, which had two of the characteristics of Christian burial – their graves were orientated east–west, and they were found with none of the grave-goods commonly associated with pagan burials. A suggested interpretation of this site is that the local landowning family to whom it belonged adopted Christianity, probably during the 340s or 350s, and so converted their temple to an estate church. Thereafter when a death occurred in the family the pagan rite was abandoned in favour of a simple Christian grave.

A more complicated – indeed, bizarre would be an apter description – Christian burial seems to have been uncovered when the site of the former Victorian workhouse at Purton, near Swindon, was being excavated in 1987-8. Archaeologists explored part of an enclosed Romano-British cemetery and found, alongside inhumations with and without stone coffins, an extraordinary cremation burial, which is now displayed in Swindon Museum. The cremated remains of a woman, together with several birds (perhaps food for the journey) were contained within a glass vessel like a small carboy; this fitted inside a cylindrical lead container, which in turn was housed in a stone casket, known as an *ossuarium*. Nothing could be more unlike the supposedly Christian burials recovered elsewhere from Roman Britain; but the lead container was decorated with a design of shells and a large saltire cross (two of the symbols of Christian allegiance) and further crosses had been incised on the lid.

This Romano-British lead cylinder, seen here as excavated at Purton in 1988, surrounded a glass vessel containing cremated human remains. One of the shells and part of a small cross scratched into the lead are visible.

Two neighbouring Roman villa-estates along Wiltshire's eastern border have also yielded ambiguous evidence which may point to a Christian presence. At Castle Copse overlooking Great Bedwyn in 1983-4 a team of American archaeologists exploring a Roman villa uncovered a mosaic pavement which included a Christian symbol, the *cantharus* or chalice. The site had been known since about 1780, and among the earliest discoveries to be made was 'a massive lead cistern', which was

The Orpheus mosaic at Littlecote Roman villa, near Ramsbury.

promptly destroyed. Roman lead tanks or cisterns, sometimes marked with Christian monograms and emblems, have been found in many parts of Britain, and are thought to have been used in Christian ritual, either for baptism or for the symbolic washing of feet. More discoveries were made in 1853, including a small gold ring, inscribed with a cross, which was donated to Devizes Museum, from where it was stolen in about 1943.

Nearby, at Littlecote, the well-known 'Orpheus' mosaic, which was lovingly excavated and restored for public inspection, appears to have been contained within a basilica-like building, set apart from the main villa-complex on the banks of the River Kennet. As such it has been suggested that it performed a religious function, but opinion is divided as to whether or not it could have been a Christian church, the figure of Orpheus symbolizing Christ.

A third villa investigation, still (2005) in progress, is potentially the most significant Roman Christian site in Wiltshire. In the grounds of St Laurence School, Bradford on Avon, a room in an opulent fourth-century villa seems to have been adapted in the fifth century for Christian ritual by the insertion of a lead tank or baptistery. It is suggested that the complex became the focus for a landowning aristocracy who, faced with the turbulent disintegration of their culture after AD 400, embraced Christianity as a way of legitimizing their position. Bradford was an important Christian centre in the Saxon period, as we shall see, and if this interpretation can be tested and confirmed, it may offer for the first time a thread of continuity extending through the Dark Ages.

Two points emerge from this review of Christian evidence from Roman Wiltshire. The first is that the outward show of Christian belief is ambiguous, enigmatic and confused – a far cry from the stalwart theologians of the fourth-century Roman empire, thinkers such as Athanasius and Augustine, who were busy defining the role of the church as the state religion, and tackling the central questions of orthodox belief. The second point is that most of what we know or surmise about Christianity in Roman Wiltshire has been discovered during the last quarter-century. The story is moving on, and we cannot afford to be dogmatic.

Despite the newly discovered Bradford baptistery it would be rash to believe that this superficial gloss of Christianity, occasionally turned up in Roman Wiltshire, could have survived

in any very meaningful way the break-up of the empire which
championed it. Like other trappings of late-Roman culture and
civilization it must have dwindled into insignificance during the
fifth and sixth centuries, to linger half-remembered alongside
the potent native godlings of stream and grove. And when
Christianity returned during the seventh century it was to places
already imbued with religious power that the missionaries sometimes turned, and chose as the sites for their Christian worship.
Evidence from all over England has been discovered of churches
and churchyards coinciding with Roman and pagan sites, and it
will be worthwhile to consider a few examples from Wiltshire.

The more discriminating visitors who explore Avebury
are attracted not only by the bewildering array of prehistoric
monuments, but also by the handsome parish church of late-
Saxon origin. Avebury (perhaps then named 'Kennet' after its

The important church at Avebury is
strategically placed just outside the
prehistoric henge monument and
stone circle.

The Bronze Age round barrow, overgrown by trees, in the churchyard at Ogbourne St Andrew, near Marlborough.

river) seems to have been chosen by the Saxons for a high-status church, which became the centre of a rural deanery and the site of a small monastic community. But the churchyard lies within a few metres of one of the most important prehistoric ritual sites in Europe, and its pagan potency was not lost on the Saxons. They called it 'Wallditch', the ditch of the natives, and named the hill which overlooks it 'Wadon', the hill of the heathens. In the middle ages they broke up and buried the magic stones.

A less well known juxtaposition of prehistoric and Christian occurs a few miles away, at Ogbourne St Andrew, near Marlborough. Here the churchyard has preserved a large bronze age round barrow, which was reused during the pagan Saxon and (Christian) medieval periods for intrusive burials. As at Avebury, one imagines, it was the religious sanctity surrounding a prehistoric monument which made it an appropriate place for a Christian church.

The Ogbourne barrow today is shrouded by trees, including a yew nearby, and examples of venerable yew trees on barrow-like mounds in churchyards are known from elsewhere in England. As a symbol of immortality the evergreen yew is appropriate to both Christian and pagan expectations of the afterlife, and it has been suggested that some churches were built next to existing 'sacred' yew trees. In Wiltshire a good candidate would be the now redundant medieval church at Alton Priors in Pewsey Vale. Here the churchyard yew is claimed to be 1,700 years old; if this is correct, it was a mature tree long before Christianity returned to Saxon Britain. A form of tree-worship may also underlie a medieval legend about St Aldhelm. At Bishopstrow ('the bishop's tree') near Warminster the site of the parish church was supposedly determined when Bishop Aldhelm preached there in the eighth century. During the

The venerable yew tree in the churchyard at Alton Priors is believed to be 1,700 years old, far more ancient than the adjacent church. If the dating is accurate it is an example not of a tree in a churchyard, but of a church in a tree-yard!

sermon, so the legend runs, his ashen staff, which he had fixed into the ground, sprouted buds and leaves, and when he had finished he left it there, where it propagated further ash trees, and gave the community its name.

Other Wiltshire churches lie on or close to the sites of Roman buildings. Part of a mosaic was discovered in 1913 under a path which led between Cherhill churchyard and manor house, near Calne, and the area was further investigated in 1984. At Box a luxurious Roman villa lay on a site a few metres north of the churchyard, overlooking the delectable valley of the By Brook, and was partially excavated in 1967-8. In 1985, after a wall collapsed between the garden of the old rectory and part of the graveyard at Manningford Bruce, near Pewsey, builders repairing it discovered part of a Roman mosaic, and an area was subsequently excavated. At Market Lavington archaeologists working on the rising ground immediately to the north-west of the churchyard have discovered settlement remains beginning in the late Roman period, and continuing through Saxon times right up to the thirteenth century. A Roman villa is known to have existed on the site of Netheravon House, near the Saxon church, and finds of Roman material have also occurred near Purton, Winterbourne Gunner, Maiden Bradley and Winterslow churches. Roman bricks were discovered in the fabric of St Mary's Church at Cricklade when it was restored in 1862.

Instances of Roman and Christian juxtaposition such as these can be explained in several ways. Some may be pure coincidence. Romans and Saxons, the argument might run, could both spot a good site for an important building, and sometimes they reached the same conclusion. Some may be pragmatism. Builders of stone churches needed a convenient supply of materials, and a derelict Roman villa would offer the ideal quarry. If the church was built next to the villa carrying costs could be kept to a minimum.

But what should we conclude when we discover that a piece of pagan Roman sculpture, such as a tombstone or altar, has been incorporated into a church? Three Wiltshire examples suggest that perhaps the church builders were conscious of the possible religious significance, and included the Roman work as a kind of talisman. The long-destroyed church at Water Eaton, near

Cricklade, boasted a font made of pieces of two massive
Roman columns, which were probably salvaged from a temple
or public building at Cirencester; they are now in Latton church
nearby. At Tockenham church near Wootton Bassett a Roman
domestic altar was built into the exterior of the south wall of
the medieval nave, and the figure carved on it came to be
identified with St Christopher. It is similar to one found at
Chedworth in Gloucestershire, and is believed to represent a
deity, or *genius*, of life and fertility. In 1900 a damaged Roman
sculpture of the goddess Fortuna was discovered to have been
concealed, probably after 1653, in the rebuilding of St Mary's
Church, Marlborough after a fire. Before that date it is assumed
that it was on public view within the church, and may have been
revered as a statue of St Catherine. Since 1900 it has again been
on view, reset at the west end of the nave near the tower arch.

Opposite: Two portions of Roman columns which were re-used as a font at Water Eaton near Cricklade, and are now in the church at Latton.

The attitude of early Saxon Christians to sites of pagan worship seems to have been that they should be adapted for Christian purposes rather than destroyed or ignored, and this is in line with the pope's instructions in AD 601 to the English missionaries. It has been suggested by Richard Morris that before about 850, 'Christianity did not so much displace pagan religion as form a kind of crust upon the surface of popular culture'. This would explain many of the examples from Wiltshire churches described above, and can perhaps be seen in the siting and early history of others.

Wroughton church occupies a commanding position overlooking the claylands of modern Swindon, on a boundary (which is recorded in about AD 956) between two estates, Ellendun and Elcombe. The names mean 'Elen's Hill' and 'Elen's Valley'. The church, which is dedicated to St John the Baptist and St Helen, overlies part of an earlier enclosure, and nearby, in 956, was a landmark described as 'Elen's Thorn'. What is intriguing about all this is that several dedications in northern England to St Helen have been linked with a Celtic deity, Elen, who was a goddess of roads and armies. Wroughton's territory, as it happens, extends up on to the downs as far as a major prehistoric highway, the Great Ridgeway. It is perhaps not too far-fetched to see at Wroughton a hilltop shrine to the pagan Elen which has been christianized into a church of St Helen. If so the old goddess still stalks the area, as she has given her name to the Ellendun shopping centre.

Opposite: A Roman domestic altar can be seen built into the exterior of Tockenham church nave.

One further consideration will take our story firmly away from Roman Britain and Dark Age paganism, and into the world of Saxon churches and their distribution. Recent thinking suggests that, prior to the widespread establishment in the later Saxon period of village communities, with open field agriculture and manorial organization, there was an earlier system of large estates. Each possessed one or more centre, which controlled smaller satellite hamlets, and these often specialized in producing a particular commodity for the whole estate. Some of these estates were successors to the territories controlled by the larger Roman villas, and retained the same boundaries. It has been suggested, for example, that two of the villas which we mentioned earlier, Castle Copse and Littlecote, were superseded by Saxon estate-centres at Great Bedwyn and Ramsbury. Box and Market Lavington may have evolved from Roman antecedents in the same way.

Above: The megalithic quoins (cornerstones) of this cottage in Westport, Malmesbury, suggest that the building began as the nave of a Saxon chapel.

Opposite: The medieval nave of Malmesbury abbey church, on the site of Mailduib's foundation, and an important focus for the evangelization of seventh-century Wessex.

Missionary activity during the seventh century reflected this arrangement of estates, so that many of the earliest churches were established at their centres, and came to act as headquarters from which priests could evangelize the outlying countryside. This, incidentally, is another reason why we should not be too surprised if we find early or important churches close to, and apparently succeeding, Roman archaeological sites. But it also offers a framework for understanding Christianity in Saxon Wiltshire. And to see it at work we should turn our attention first to Malmesbury.

An Irish monk or hermit named Mailduib, according to legend, settled in a remote, wooded area of north Wiltshire in about 637, and attracted a small community of pupils around him. This was the origin of Malmesbury, which under Mailduib's successor, Aldhelm, became one of the most important Christian sites in Wessex.

Between 680 and 701 kings and noblemen gave land along the Gloucestershire–Wiltshire border to this community, and the area, we must assume, was evangelized by the brethren. Certainly by the end of the Saxon period stone churches had been built in several of the nearby villages controlled by Malmesbury Abbey. The tall, thin walls of Crudwell's nave appear to be Saxon in origin; at Westport the nave of a Saxon church has recently been discovered in use as a private house; and at Somerford Keynes (now in Gloucestershire) the surviving Saxon doorway is considered by many to date from Aldhelm's time. It is perhaps no coincidence that a medieval legend, recounted by John Aubrey, attributed to Aldhelm the discovery of Hazelbury freestone quarry, near Box. In some, perhaps most, instances stone churches replaced earlier timber structures, and at Bremilham (Cowage Farm), 3 km west of Malmesbury, remains of such a building were discovered by aerial photography in 1975, and later excavated. Another vanished building is suggested by the name Whitchurch, on Malmesbury's northern outskirts. Although not recorded until the thirteenth century, the name has been found elsewhere to denote a new stone-built church during the later Saxon period. Malmesbury's Whitchurch survived as a chapel until the seventeenth century.

The work of Aldhelm and his colleagues was not restricted to the Malmesbury area. We have already referred to his preaching activities at Bishopstrow, near Warminster, and we know too that he established communities at Bradford on Avon and Frome (Somerset). Bradford is a good example of a large Saxon estate, perhaps inherited from the Budbury Roman villa on the hillside above the town, which continued as a medieval administrative unit known as a hundred. The Saxon missionaries therefore adopted the same territory, with their headquarters probably on the site of the present parish church (Holy Trinity), and preaching stations established in the outlying settlements. In due course each was given its own permanent place of worship, but they remained chapels-of-ease dependent on the mother-church in Bradford itself. One of these chapels, Limpley Stoke, retains part of its Saxon nave and a doorway; two others, Atworth and Holt, are recorded in documents soon after the conquest; and several others retain medieval fabric, including Winsley, South Wraxall, and St Mary Tory, above Bradford town. Further daughter chapels are believed to have existed at Ashley, Barley and Cumberwell, and in Bradford itself.

Also in Bradford, close to the parish church, lay the famous chapel of St Laurence. This was perhaps built in about 1001 to house the relics of St Edward the Martyr, which were to be moved there for safe keeping from Shaftesbury. Concealed by buildings it was revealed as one of England's most complete Saxon churches during the nineteenth century.

The premises of evangelizing priests at the centre of secular estates were known as minsters, and their existence is known, or can be deduced, at various places in Wiltshire.

This narrow Saxon doorway at Limpley Stoke has been retained as part of the south arcade.

Warminster carries this information in its name, and several
other towns – like Warminster centres of medieval hundreds –
probably also had minsters. Examples include Calne, Westbury,

Opposite: St Laurence's Chapel, Bradford on Avon, one of the most complete Saxon churches in southern England, owes its preservation to its having been concealed among other buildings, and 'lost' until the nineteenth century.

Below: Elaborate carving on the jamb of a Saxon doorway in the former minster church at Britford.

Melksham and Amesbury. But not all minster centres would today be recognized as towns. Heytesbury, Great Bedwyn, Upavon and Ramsbury are all now larger-than-average villages, but Avebury, Winterbourne Stoke (near Shrewton), Britford and Alderbury (both near Salisbury) have remained small.

No systematic attempt has yet been made to plot all Wiltshire's minsters with their dependent territories, but evidence of their activities has survived in various ways. Some, like Bradford, Westbury and Bedwyn, retained through the middle ages a number of chapels-of-ease within large parishes. Some are recorded in Domesday Book as having churches with substantial landholdings attached to them; these include Avebury, Heytesbury, Highworth and Upavon. Sometimes a stray reference provides the clue. The cure of a hunchbacked priest at the shrine of St Swithun in Winchester was celebrated in a tenth-century poem; the priest, it tells us, was attached to the king's headquarters (*villa regalis*) at Alderbury. From this we may deduce that he belonged to the minster established at the centre of the royal estate of Alderbury.

More tangible evidence, in the form of sculpture and surviving buildings, permits us to glimpse the system at work. The minster church itself might have been a substantial stone building ornamented with rich decoration. At Britford much of the Saxon nave is preserved, along with openings into side chapels; the jamb of the northern opening has intricate vine-scroll decoration. At Netheravon the probable minster church has a massive foursquare Saxon tower.

A blocked opening into a vanished chamber, or *porticus*, can be seen at the base of Netheravon's late-Saxon tower.

This masterpiece of Saxon art, the cross shaft at Codford St Peter, portrays a figure which may have pagan, rather than Christian, connotations.

From such centres priests toured the countryside, preaching and conducting services. Their regular preaching stations were marked originally by crosses, and these were sometimes preserved in or around the churches which eventually replaced them. The most notable Saxon cross shaft in Wiltshire is in the chancel at Codford St Peter near Warminster, and may depict 'the archer in the vine'. This motif, representing Christ in union with his church, is based on the passage in St John chapter 15 beginning, 'I am the true vine', and is linked with the trees of the Lord in Psalm 104. An alternative identification is with a pagan fertility god, Sucellos, whose emblem was a mallet. Other carved Saxon crosses are at Colerne, Ramsbury and Amesbury, and there are fragments elsewhere. Plainer crosses of indeterminate date exist in many churchyards and elsewhere – at Ashton Keynes the village boasts four crosses. In addition two place-names appear to be describing Saxon crosses: Croucheston in the Ebble valley is 'the farm by the cross'; and Christian Malford is 'the ford by the crucifix (*cristel-mael*)'.

The next stage in the process was the building, generally by a local landowner, of a 'field-church' (sometimes known as a 'proprietary' church) for his own and his tenants' use. It is likely that most medieval parish churches which had not been minsters began life in this way, and we have already discussed how sometimes their sites may have been chosen on the basis of previous pagan worship. At Bremilham we mentioned a timber church of this sort, and excavations at Potterne have revealed another wooden proprietary church, which seems to have included not only a nave and chancel, but also a baptistery and a house for the priest. The Saxon font which presumably occupied the baptistery is now in the parish church; it has an inscription in Latin from Psalm 42.

Information about wooden churches is scarce, because in most cases it is likely that they were destroyed and replaced by stone structures on the same site. Likewise the earliest stonebuilt phase of many later parish churches has disappeared or been disguised by subsequent alterations and rebuildings. Survival of late-Saxon proprietary churches is most likely when the community which they served remained small throughout the middle ages, and failed to prosper. Examples of Saxon evidence in small Wiltshire churches, such as windows, doorways, pilaster strips or megalithic quoining, are to be found at Alton Barnes in Pewsey Vale, at Burcombe near Wilton, Knook near Warminster, and Inglesham beside the Thames, opposite Lechlade.

The hierarchy of minsters and proprietary churches was essentially a rural one. In those towns established during the later Saxon period which had not previously been estate centres a slightly different pattern emerged. Here the equivalent of the field-church was the small privately-owned church serving a few streets or a section of the population. In Wiltshire only at Wilton did such a proliferation of urban churches take place (at least eight by the medieval period, and four in the suburbs), and no Saxon fabric survives, but Old Sarum boasted four churches in the twelfth century, and Cricklade and Marlborough each had two important churches before 1100. At Cricklade the

The Saxon font at Potterne, with Latin inscription around its rim, may once have been housed in a wooden precursor of the present church in which it stands.

principal church, St Sampson's, retains Saxon work, and St Mary's (now Catholic) is to be found at one of the characteristic positions of churches in planned Saxon towns, next to a gateway. A Saxon gateway church survives at Wareham (Dorset), and a church of Holy Cross is known to have been incorporated into Old Sarum's east gate. On Chisbury, a remote hillfort overlooking Savernake Forest, there is evidence that a small fortified town was laid out in the ninth century. None of it survives, but there is the shell of a medieval chapel next to the hillfort's east gate, and it is quite possible that this replaced a Saxon predecessor on the same site.

As we bring to an end this brief survey of Roman and Saxon Christianity in Wiltshire, it is important to notice that one word has been almost entirely absent from our discussion. That word is 'parish', and it is with the formation of parishes and the creation of parish churches that our next chapter should begin.

Chisbury, near Great Bedwyn, is a hillfort reused in the Saxon period. Its medieval thatched chapel, of which the shell is preserved, adjoins the site of the east gate, and may have replaced a Saxon original.

22

The Parish Church takes shape

MONEY AND TERRITORY are not the words which first spring to mind when thinking about medieval parish churches. Yet they are the keys to understanding how and why parishes came into being. The Saxon minsters and monasteries which spearheaded the christianization of Wiltshire were supported by endowments of land donated by benefactors. Indeed, we have already noticed that in Domesday Book possession of land by a church may be taken as one piece of evidence that it began life as a minster. And the proprietary or field-churches which sprang up as a result of the minster-priests' activities were supported by the estate owners who built them, and who viewed them perhaps as an accoutrement, much as we might regard a swimming-pool or tennis court in the garden of a superior residence. For this reason churches close to manor houses are often assumed to

Opposite: Potterne church presides over its village. The estate of Potterne belonged to the bishops of Salisbury, and the architecture of this fine church has close affinities with Salisbury Cathedral.

have been proprietary in origin. But during the tenth century, when evangelism was turning to consolidation, this reliance on patronage and benefaction was augmented by a new source of income, the Biblical notion of tithes.

The idea that everyone should pay one-tenth of their income to support the church and its priests was not imposed universally overnight, but as it came to be adopted – from the mid-tenth century onwards – there was an obvious need to define responsibilities. To which priest should an individual pay tithes and dues, and to whom should that priest minister? Thus each church was seen to have its own territory, and everyone living within its boundaries owed allegiance to that church alone. In practice the adaptation of one system of government, the minster, to another, the parish, was achieved in a gradual, piecemeal and awkward fashion.

Saxon secular administration seems to have been based on a decimal system, with hamlet or village units known as tithings grouped into larger territories called hundreds. In theory ten hides or ten households made a tithing, and ten tithings made a hundred; but by the end of the Saxon period centuries of adaptation had already blurred this neat definition, and further changes occurred after the conquest. For the church, however, here was a ready-made system of administrative boundaries (sometimes, in fact, Roman or even prehistoric in origin) which could be taken over and modified to suit particular circumstances. And this link forged between tithings, hundreds and parishes was the more natural – almost inevitable, one might suggest – because of two further factors. In the first place many of the Saxon minsters had been established at hundredal centres, as we have seen, and regarded the hundred as their sphere of activity. And in the second place the field-churches were built by landowners whose property generally coincided with one or more tithings.

The process whereby, over two or more centuries, certain field-churches became parochial, while others remained subordinate to their former minsters, is not, for the most part, recorded, nor are all the power struggles, disputes and ill feelings which this rearrangement must have engendered. We are presented with a medieval *fait accompli*, of parish churches and chapels-of-ease, and can only glimpse vestiges of the earlier system. Various permutations were possible, and are best illustrated by examples.

The parish of Dauntsey presides over part of the flat clay valley of the Bristol Avon which is now traversed by the M4 between Chippenham and Swindon. In the year 850 a ten-hide estate (probably therefore a tithing) called Dauntsey was given by the king to Malmesbury Abbey, and it was one of the many endowments of land which the abbey retained as overlord until its dissolution. The tithing's boundaries were described in the 850 grant, and, with the addition of a small estate called Smithcot during the middle ages, and a few other minor

Enford, a fine Norman and later building, which succeeded in becoming the parish church for no fewer than six tithings.

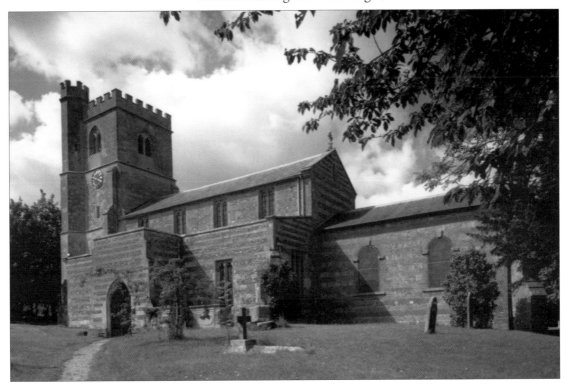

alterations, they became the boundaries of the ecclesiastical parish and continued virtually unaltered until it was united with its neighbour Brinkworth in 1961. It has been suggested that Dauntsey church was built by Malmesbury Abbey before the conquest; it would therefore have begun as a proprietary church, provided for his tenants by the landowner, the abbot. Its position close to Dauntsey House, the probable successor to the first manor house, tends to confirm this suggestion. Since Malmesbury Abbey, Dauntsey's minster centre and mother

St Mary's, Old Dilton remained a chapel-of-ease to Westbury until the nineteenth century. When Dilton was finally given parochial status a new church was built at Dilton Marsh, where most of the parishioners lived.

church, continued to own it and would profit from its tithes, there was presumably no opposition to Dauntsey becoming an autonomous parish, although by the thirteenth century Malmesbury had lost direct control of the church. Smithcot, a separate estate in Domesday Book (1086), had its own place of worship during the fourteenth and fifteenth centuries, but because by then it lay within Dauntsey parish it was only a chapel-of-ease, and never achieved autonomy.

In Dauntsey, therefore (and the same story could be told of many other Wiltshire places), there seems to have been almost the simplest possible progression: from tithing and proprietary church, to parish and parish church. Only Smithcot complicates the issue. But by contrast at both Bishopstone, in the Ebble valley west of Salisbury, and Enford, on Salisbury Plain, groups of no fewer than six adjacent tithings were formed into single parishes, which took their names from where their churches stood. Neither began as a Saxon minster. Bishopstone was probably still being served by priests from the minster at Downton as late as 1086, and it has been suggested that the present church may have been begun soon afterwards at the same time as the parish was created. Enford was probably one of a number of field-churches within a hundred known as Elstub, which had its minster centre at Netheravon. From medieval references to churches and chapels it appears that, as the minster's influence dwindled, these churches broke away. Fittleton and Haxton formed one parish, with its parish church at Fittleton and a chapel-of-ease at Haxton. Enford, with dependent chapels at Compton and Coombe, and perhaps also in one or more of its other tithings, formed another parish. Netheravon retained its hold over one chapelry, at West Chisenbury, even though this lay some 5km away, beyond Enford.

The contrasting fortunes of the former minsters are well illustrated in west Wiltshire. One of them, Westbury, managed to retain its whole territory as a single parish until the nineteenth century. Only then were its ancient chapelries of Bratton and Dilton given parochial status, a new parish and church were made for Heywood, and chapels-of-ease were built at Chapmanslade and Westbury Leigh. Bradford minster, too, held on to most of its dependencies, and even some which did achieve parochial status, such as Broughton Gifford and Great Chalfield, were at times referred to as 'chapels'. Melksham saw four of its constituents, including Hilperton and

Trowbridge, break away and form parishes, but it retained Seend and Erlestoke as chapelries. Warminster's territory seems to have fragmented into parishes at an early date; only Corsley remained a chapelry, and in 1415 it too began to take on one of the parochial responsibilities, that of burying its own dead.

It must be clear from this attempt to describe it that the process of parish formation was piecemeal, haphazard and inconsistent, and that it led to unevenness in church funding and provision. Untidy it may be, but we have had to labour the

Great Chalfield wrested its parochial autonomy from the mother church at Bradford on Avon, although in appearance it remained the chapel of an important house, and was sometimes so regarded.

point because of its obvious bearing on the number and quality of medieval churches which were built and rebuilt as a result. (Another, less obvious, consequence will become apparent when we consider the emergence of nonconformity many centuries later.)

Tithe and other payments generated a reliable and substantial income for the new parish churches and their manorial owners, although as the middle ages wore on an increasing proportion was siphoned off by monasteries, the cathedral, and other religious foundations. This process, known as appropriation, will be discussed in the next chapter. But in the eleventh and twelfth centuries money was clearly available for a massive church-building campaign, and proprietary owners enlarged their churches or built anew – much as they might rebuild the manorial mill – as a form of investment. 'Churches rise in every village', wrote a monk of Malmesbury, the historian William, in about 1125. This was the period (especially between about 1050 and 1150) when most of the remaining wooden field churches which we encountered in the last chapter were replaced by stone buildings. A dilapidated wooden chapel at Knook, near Heytesbury, recorded in 1226, may have been one of the last survivors.

Guidebooks customarily talk about 'a fourteenth-century church', or 'the church dates from the Early English period', as if it was new, or entirely rebuilt, at this period. Entirely new churches were built, of course, at most periods, but this was not common. Usually the guidebook should be interpreted as meaning that the earliest datable features (such as windows, doors or arches) reflect a particular period. Archaeological interest in churches during the past thirty years has demonstrated time and again that a long sequence of building phases is to be found in most churches, and the concept of a 'nest' or 'stack' of churches occupying the same site has been put forward. Very often a Saxon wooden phase (undetectable now except by excavation) was replaced by a stonebuilt Norman church, which was then subjected to successive additions, modifications and repairs throughout the middle ages. Two examples will suffice.

Turning gratefully off the A36 at Stapleford in the Wylye valley one passes first the cottage where Vaughan Williams composed part of his fifth symphony, and then sees the church ahead, framed by a row of cottages and a high grass bank. A squat battlemented tower peers from behind the high nave roof, below which protrudes a substantial porch. There are windows of various dates, styles and sizes. Clearly this church has a complicated building history. In fact careful analysis has revealed five medieval building phases, as well as a seventeenth-century upper stage on the tower and two Victorian restorations. A simple rectangular nave with small, almost square, chancel of about 1125 was enlarged about fifty years later by the building of a south aisle. The resulting late-Norman arcade, with dogtooth and chevron patterns, is the most memorable feature of the interior. Then, in about 1250 the chancel was enlarged and a north chapel built. A century or so later alterations were made to the chancel, a tower was built against the nave north wall, and a chapel with a fine south window was made in the south aisle. The south porch was added in the mid-fifteenth century.

Various factors may underlie all these adaptations: the changing fashions of the times; the desire to keep a church large enough for parish needs in good repair; developments in the liturgy and ritual practised within it; modifications encouraged by the diocesan authorities. But especially important seem to have been the changes in ownership and control (and consequently in attitudes and funding) which occurred during the period. Stapleford church was given to Old Sarum Cathedral by Henry I (who reigned 1100-35), and so this may be the context for the first building phase now recognizable – presumably there was an earlier wooden or stonebuilt church of which no trace remains above ground. By 1226 the church had passed out of the cathedral's hands, and by 1300 the patron was a member of the Esturmy family. The substantial thirteenth- and fourteenth-century additions were perhaps, therefore, the work of this wealthy and influential Wiltshire dynasty. Then in 1444 Stapleford was appropriated by Easton Priory, near Pewsey, and at about this time the new porch was built.

A similar analysis has helped to unravel the history of Compton Bassett church, near Calne. Here part of a sarsen stone wall, believed to have belonged to a Saxon church later demolished, has been discovered. It was incorporated into a Victorian coal cellar when the chancel was rebuilt and the church restored in 1866. After this Saxon phase the sequence is similar to that at Stapleford. A simple Norman church was extended by building first a north and later a south

This notable south arcade was part of the late-Norman contribution to Stapleford's multi-period church

aisle. Then, in the fourteenth and fifteenth centuries, a new chancel arch with stairway to a rood loft was added, followed by the usual Perpendicular west tower. Some rebuilding and a new porch have been dated to the eighteenth century, and thoroughgoing Victorian restoration replaced the small Norman chancel, which is now only known from an earlier painting. The fine late-medieval screen of Caen stone in front of the chancel arch appears too grand for a remote country church, and does not seem to have been designed to fit the space which it now

Compton Bassett's carved
Caen stone screen appears not
to have been purpose-made,
but was probably brought from
elsewhere.

Opposite: Earthworks of a
vanished settlement greet the
visitor to the remote and
minuscule church of Buttermere
on the Berkshire border.

occupies. Perhaps, the author of the study suggests, it came from a dissolved monastery, or much later from a cathedral during restoration.

Close examination of churches such as Stapleford and Compton Bassett is a rewarding exercise, not least because it reveals the complexity and dynamism of the parish church as an archaeological and historic monument. It is a kind of barometer of the community it has served, reflecting in its architecture the times of poverty and prosperity, expansion and retrenchment. To write the biography of a church in this way, therefore, is to probe also the lives of its parishioners, especially those with the power and the money to effect change.

Stapleford and Compton Bassett are typical of very many parish churches, but by no means all. Sometimes too few people or too little money meant that the church never progressed far beyond its first stonebuilt phase, a square or apsidal chancel attached to a simple rectangular nave. They are unsung, these little churches, but few visitors fail to be moved by Fifield Bavant, for example, or Rollestone, or Buttermere, or – best of all – Manningford Bruce. Here the church, with its chancel apse and its herringbone flintwork, is still essentially a small Norman field-church of about 1100. At Buttermere, in that remote downland country where Wiltshire,

The small apsidal Norman church of Manningford Bruce was sympathetically restored in 1882. The chancel ceiling of parquet blocks imitates the exterior flintwork which was laid in herringbone fashion.

Hampshire and Berkshire meet, the reason for the church's modest dimensions are apparent as soon as one approaches; for in the field sloping down towards it are the earthwork remains of the village which once it served.

We are fortunate that such parish churches have survived, because they illustrate a stage beyond which most of their counterparts elsewhere evolved. But in any evolutionary theory there must be losers as well as winners, and it is hardly surprising that the buildings most vulnerable to extinction through impecunity and neglect were those which never achieved parochial status, the medieval chapels-of-ease. Great Bedwyn's stately parish church is almost certainly successor to a minster whose sparsely populated territory embraced much of Savernake Forest. Of its dependencies Burbage achieved parish status by the twelfth century, and Little Bedwyn in the fifteenth. Both are interesting churches preserving work of several periods. But four other villages and hamlets were served only by medieval chapels, which all subsequently fell out of religious use. Two, at East Grafton and Marten, disappeared completely and were forgotten, until their foundations were uncovered by the Victorians, in 1844 and 1858 respectively. The two others, at Knowle and Chisbury, were put to use as farm buildings, and their shells survive. The little thatched chapel at Chisbury is an evocative place. Approached through a farmyard, it stands beside the entrance to an iron-age hillfort, gazing out across the wooded landscape of eastern Wiltshire.

A similar tale of disused and disappearing chapels could be told of the territory of Frustfield or Whiteparish, along the road from Salisbury to Romsey; here too (at Whelpley) part of a chapel has survived, because it was put to use as a farm building. At least three other chapels in Whiteparish have vanished. In west Wiltshire two chapels seem to have been abandoned, at Coople and Baynton, when their respective parish churches — Keevil and Edington — were rebuilt. And on the Marlborough Downs the medieval churches at Draycot Foliat and Shaw suffered the same fate as their villages, which dwindled to nothing. In both cases some of their masonry is thought to have been robbed for reuse in the parish churches which took over their territories, Chiseldon and Alton Barnes respectively.

Against this undercurrent of failure should be set the impressive achievements of medieval architects and masons elsewhere in Wiltshire. From each of the four medieval periods and styles which were first distinguished by Thomas Rickman in 1817, and which every church visitor carries around in his or her head – Norman, Early English, Decorated and Perpendicular – Wiltshire has preserved major examples. The splendour of Malmesbury's Norman nave, the consummation of Early English purity at Salisbury Cathedral, and the exquisite transition from Decorated to Perpendicular at Edington will all reappear in the next chapter, when we discuss specialist churches. At parish level a series of piecemeal enlargements was the norm, as we have seen, but there are also a few examples to be enjoyed of large and expensive building projects resulting in new or entirely remodelled medieval churches.

Devizes did not exist until about 1100, when a major castle was begun on the hillside overlooking the claylands of west Wiltshire. A semi-circular bailey was laid out, and a chapel dedicated to St John was built on the grand scale to serve the castle community. A new town developed, describing an arc outside the curving bailey wall, and St Mary's church was built next to its first market place (hence Maryport). Later the town expanded into the bailey, and the chapel became a second parish church. Both churches have kept their fine Norman chancels, and St John's its massive crossing tower, but as might be expected in a successful medieval town, the naves of both were renewed in the fifteenth century.

Opposite: The sturdy tower of St John's Church, Devizes, which was built as the chapel of the important Norman castle.

One does not have to stray far from Devizes to find the two best examples in Wiltshire of Early English parish churches. Devizes had been created by a bishop of Salisbury at the boundary (hence the name) of two large rural estates which he owned, Potterne and Bishop's Cannings. It was episcopal money, therefore, which determined the architecture of their churches. Both were comprehensively rebuilt at around the time that Salisbury Cathedral was being created, and comparisons are frequently drawn. Bishop's Cannings is a little earlier than the cathedral, with which its architectural detail has less in common than Potterne. But because it has a (much later) spire, whereas Potterne has only a tower, Bishop's Cannings is sometimes regarded as Salisbury Cathedral in miniature. Potterne, in fact, is

The church of Bishop's Cannings, an episcopal manor as its name suggests, is sometimes regarded as a miniature Salisbury Cathedral, and its spire is a notable landmark in the Vale of Pewsey.

much closer in both date and architectural detail to the cathedral, and only the decorative battlements on the tower are later (see page 22).

A tax assessed and levied nationally in 1334 placed Wiltshire fourth in the ranking of English counties, wealthier than everywhere except Norfolk, Kent and Gloucestershire. During the following two centuries Wiltshire's capital, Salisbury, grew on the back of its cloth industry to become one of the largest cities in England, and the towns and villages of west Wiltshire in particular discovered prosperity from their own burgeoning woollen trade. It was time to do something about the church. Many strands of motivation have been suggested to account for the flowering of Perpendicular architecture during the later fourteenth and fifteenth centuries. Simple gratitude for divine mercy and munificence, leading to a desire to lavish money on the house of God, is an important factor in the equation. A more complicated religious explanation involves the growing belief in the efficacy of prayers for the dead, through chantries and guilds, and hence the wish to 'buy' salvation by contributing to the fabric of churches where such prayers would be said. This will be discussed in chapter four. More mundane explanations involve simple expansion to accommodate a growing population, the perennial necessity to repair or replace decrepitude, and competition between one community and its neighbour, each striving to outdo the other.

In Wiltshire the finest examples of Perpendicular parish churches are to be found in Salisbury (St Thomas's), in the

Opposite: Steeple Ashton is the showpiece among Wiltshire's late-medieval churches. The tower was surmounted by a spire until it fell in 1670.

The interior of Steeple Ashton church is as glorious as its exterior. After its stone vault was destroyed by the falling spire the nave was given a wooden ceiling.

other clothing towns, such as Trowbridge, Calne, Westbury and Bradford, and in many of the larger villages of west and north-west Wiltshire. Lacock, Castle Combe and Keevil spring to mind, but the outstanding church is Steeple Ashton, near Trowbridge. Between 1480 and about 1510 the entire church, apart from the chancel and west tower, was built to a magnificent design at the expense of two clothiers — who each paid for an aisle — and the other parishioners, who were responsible for the nave and a spire to surmount the tower. The spire was struck twice by lightning in 1670 and collapsed; it brought down the stone vault, which was subsequently replaced in wood; the chancel was rebuilt in 1853. Nor was rebuilding towards the end of the middle ages restricted to parish churches. The chapels-of-ease at both Bratton and Seend are Perpendicular in character, the latter with an aisle erected by a clothier, John Stokes, who included his sheep-shears in the decoration.

 The striving to keep up with fashion and to compete with one's neighbours is best seen in the building of towers. Church towers may always have been a matter of prestige rather than mere utility. In the Saxon period, it has been suggested, proprietors built towers as a sign of their own power, and sometimes as a 'strong house' for defence. Netheravon's gaunt Saxon tower may be such an edifice (see page 18), and if the idea is carried forward beyond the

Clothier's shears adorn the exterior west wall of the north aisle of Seend church to indicate the source of the wealth which paid for it.

conquest we may compare the crude bulk of nearby Bulford's Norman tower with the much more sophisticated, but no less solid tower of Devizes St John, which proclaims for all to see the castle-builder's power. Similar pretensions may have motivated whichever member of the St Quintin family was responsible for the Norman tower at Stanton St Quintin, near Chippenham.

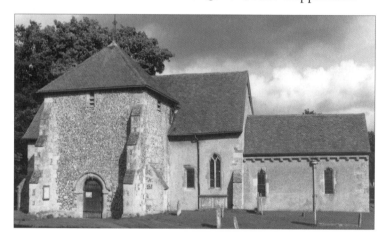

Bulford's gaunt Norman tower seems to have been designed for defence rather than worship.

But it was in the fifteenth century that tower-building reached its pinnacle, and the vogue for adding Perpendicular west towers to existing churches became widespread in Wiltshire, as also in its prosperous neighbours, Somerset and Gloucestershire. Although the motive in many cases was simply swagger, a desire to install new bell-frames which swung, rather than simply tolled, the bells, may have prompted some tower-building. In common with other adornments of the period the cost of a new tower was often underwritten by the bequests and gifts of individual parishioners. Henry Berwyk, for example, in his will of 1406, left 20 marks (about £13), 'to the building of a tower over the church of Bishopstone [near Salisbury], when the parishioners of the same begin to build it anew'. Perhaps the most elegant of Wiltshire's towers is to be found at Westwood, near Bradford, staring across to Somerset, both

The last flowering of Perpendicular elegance is seen in this Somerset-style tower at Westwood, the gift of a Tudor clothier.

literally and stylistically. It was the gift of a local clothier, Thomas Horton, who lived in the nearby manor house and died in 1530; his initials are over the church door. Its intricate blind panelling spawned imitations. Three churches in north-west Wiltshire – Nettleton, West Kington and Yatton Keynell – seem to have been inspired by it, or by its Somerset counterparts. The same motif could be used to evoke power rather than grace. The tower of St Sampson's at Cricklade is anything but graceful; but across a wide tract of the upper Thames valley its ribbed masonry and conical spirelets are an unmistakeable landmark. And taken to extremes the tower-building mania resulted in two north Wiltshire curiosities, the churches at Purton and Wanborough. Both have attractive central fourteenth-century towers surmounted by spires; but

St Mary's, Purton, claims to be one of only three churches to boast a tower and a spire. Wanborough, its near neighbour, and Ormskirk in Lancashire make up the trio.

both also have Perpendicular towers added a century or so later at the west ends of their respective naves.

Such incongruities carry us on to the last topic which this chapter must address, the duality of medieval churches, as seen in the architecture of the nave compared with that of the chancel. And, of course, the reason for it – the tension between the providers and recipients of religion, the recipients and providers of tithes.

During the middle ages it became established that the rector, or his patron, was responsible for the upkeep of the chancel, and the parishioners were responsible for the nave. Dean Chandler, when he visited Wilsford church, near Salisbury, in 1405, noted in his register that the chancel roof was defective through the rector's fault, and the nave roof was defective through the fault of the parish. Three years later, when he visited again, the chancel roof was still defective, and now the parishioners claimed that a window in the chancel was defective too, through the rector's fault. At the next visitation, in 1412, we are hardly surprised to learn that the chancel was still defective through the rector's fault; but now the tower walls too were ruinous, through the fault of the parish. Each time fresh arrangements were made for repairs, with the threat of penalties if they were neglected. Each time, it seems, very little happened.

The obvious consequence of this division of responsibilities was that east and west in many churches developed or decayed along separate lines. At Steeple Ashton, we recall, the parishioners left the chancel alone when they rebuilt the nave and aisles. At Devizes St Mary the chancel is Norman, but the nave is Perpendicular. At Urchfont in Pewsey Vale the rector was admonished in 1302 for the poor state of the chancel, and seems to have embarked on a lavish rebuilding programme which resulted in the chancel's fine Decorated lierne vault. Thereafter much of the remainder of the church was renewed, presumably by the parish.

The separate evolution of chancel and nave is best seen in the work of John Buckler, whose series of water-colours of Wiltshire churches as they appeared in the early-nineteenth century portrays many examples of awkward juxtapositions, discontinuous roof lines, badly matched materials, and the like. Orcheston St Mary and South Newton are two of many

When, in 1302, St Mary's nunnery
in Winchester was criticized for the
poor state in which it maintained
the chancel at Urchfont, it
embarked on a lavish
reconstruction which resulted in this
fine vaulted ceiling.

instances where the chancel roof protruded above the line of
the nave. The Victorian restorers removed most such anomalies
(although Wootton Bassett still suffers from this ungainly
arrangement), and in some cases chose to preserve only the

chancel, demolishing the nave or leaving it in ruins, while selecting a site for a new church elsewhere. Examples include Chitterne St Mary, Swindon Holy Rood, and Wilton St Mary.

The architectural duality, still discernible in some parish churches, may be linked to a wider duality in medieval religion, between the laity – the ordinary parishioners who worshipped in church and chapel – and the specialists, the clergy and monastic communities, who worshipped apart. The link between the two was forged, on the one hand, by the cathedral's diocesan hierarchy which controlled parish worship; but it was fostered also by the monasteries and other religious communities, who through appropriation had acquired a financial interest in the tithes of no fewer than 113 Wiltshire parishes by the time of the dissolution. The process whereby the cathedral and the monasteries came to affect parish life is one of the themes of the next chapter, which explores the architecture and society of the specialist church.

The Specialist Church

L
ET US IMAGINE that, on her way home from Canterbury in the 1390s, Chaucer's Wife of Bath found herself on the road between Ramsbury and Marlborough. Sat easily on her ambling horse she would have passed Ramsbury parish church, and perhaps been told that it stood on the site of a cathedral. In the churchyard she may have seen the prebendal house, the home of a canon of Salisbury, whose cathedral was Ramsbury's successor. The Bishop of Salisbury still owned the manor, and as she left the little town she would have crossed the park where he hunted, and passed the palace where he regularly went to stay.

Riding along Marlborough High Street she would have seen not only the two fine parish churches, but also a humbler group of buildings, the chapel and lodgings of a community of white, or Carmelite, friars, who had set up residence there some

Opposite: Salisbury Cathedral, the chancel, with ambulatory and Trinity Chapel beyond.

eighty years earlier. Had she gone down to water her horse in the Kennet she would have discovered near the bridge two more religious foundations, hospitals dedicated to St Thomas and St John, each with its own chapel. St Thomas's, between London Road and the river, cared for lepers, and in 1393 control of it passed to yet another institution, the Gilbertine priory of St Margaret, which stood nearby, at the foot of the road to Savernake and Salisbury. A few kilometres further along that road, at Easton, there was another monastery, a house of Maturin, or Trinitarian, friars, one of whose responsibilities was the succour of travellers such as herself.

But the Wife of Bath would presumably have headed westward, depending on the season taking either the valley route up the Kennet, or across Fyfield and Overton Downs to Avebury. If the former, she might have glanced across to Clatford, where a French Benedictine abbey had a small priory or grange; if the latter she would have passed quite close to another, more important, grange – at Ogbourne St George – before arriving in Temple Rockley. This, she might have been told, had belonged to the Knights Templars, and they had built a monastic house known as a preceptory there, probably with a circular church. But the quasi-religious Templars had been abolished eighty years earlier, and their lands had been given over to their arch-rivals, the Knights Hospitallers.

Eventually, after traversing downland which belonged variously to Stanley Abbey (a Cistercian house near Calne), St Margaret's Priory at Marlborough, the nuns of Wilton Abbey, and the monks of St Swithun's (the cathedral priory at Winchester), she would have dropped down to Avebury. Here, close to the parish church (controlled by Cirencester Abbey), stood yet another monastic grange, which its French owners were planning (unsuccessfully, as it turned out) to sell to Winchester College.

And none of this would have appeared at all unusual to the Wife of Bath. She was, according to Chaucer, a seasoned traveller; everywhere she went, in town and country, she would have found a rich diversity of religious houses, and monastic control over land and worship. The point, as every pilgrim would have known, was simply that medieval Christianity was not restricted to the parish church. Wiltshire alone had nearly fifty religious houses; in its time it had

Stanley Abbey was one of the many religious houses which owned land on the Marlborough Downs. This dilapidated farmhouse, close to the site of the vanished abbey, was part of the monastic complex.

come within the jurisdiction of bishops based in no fewer than five places (Dorchester-on-Thames, Sherborne, Ramsbury, Old Sarum and Salisbury – perhaps also Winchester and Wilton); and by the end of the middle ages not far short of one-half of its parish churches had been appropriated – that is, brought under the control of a monastery, other religious foundation, or cathedral official. Their landholdings were prodigious.

The largest, most opulent, and most important religious building in the Wiltshire of Chaucer's day was of course

Salisbury Cathedral. It was the headquarters of a bishop whose diocese embraced the whole of Wiltshire, as well as two neighbouring counties, Berkshire and Dorset. Like Wells and Exeter, but unlike Gloucester and Winchester, it was a secular cathedral, which meant that no community of monks was attached to it. Instead it was surrounded by the houses of its four senior officials – dean, chancellor, treasurer and precentor – and its forty-eight 'secular' canons, who formed its chapter. They in turn employed priests or scholars, known as the vicars choral, to take part in cathedral services in their absence, for many canons were not normally resident. Alongside them the medieval cathedral and close swarmed with chaplains, chantry priests, altarists and choristers.

The cathedral oversaw its diocese in much the same way as the Saxon minsters had overseen their smaller territories before the advent of the parish system. Just as Mailduib had his group of disciples evangelizing Saxon north Wiltshire from

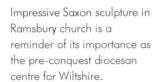

Impressive Saxon sculpture in Ramsbury church is a reminder of its importance as the pre-conquest diocesan centre for Wiltshire.

Malmesbury, so the medieval bishop at Salisbury had his 'family' of canons ostensibly looking after the spiritual welfare of three counties. And this analogy of the cathedral as a glorified minster is a useful one, because the seats of Saxon bishops were known as head minsters, and it was from them that many of the medieval cathedrals evolved. At York and Lincoln the connection is maintained by the name, and in Salisbury there survives a Minster Street to remind us that our cathedral too was formerly (and anachronistically) so described.

The office of bishop originated in the early church, and we have already referred to the existence of bishops in Roman Britain. The Saxon bishops were powerful evangelists, and advocates of the church in the courts of kings; but they also had the more humdrum rôles of supervising the priesthood and laity in their dioceses, and of consecrating new churches. Until the year 909 we cannot be certain that any bishop had his seat in Wiltshire. In that year the two dioceses which controlled Wessex, based on Winchester and Sherborne, were divided into five, with new centres at Crediton, Wells and Ramsbury. Wiltshire and Berkshire lay within the diocese of Ramsbury, which thus became a head minster or cathedral. Geographically Ramsbury was a good choice, since it lay almost on the boundary between the two counties; it was also one of five estates, the profits from which were used to endow the new bishopric. Nothing of the Saxon cathedral remains to be seen, although in the parish church, which is believed to occupy the same site, are some ornate fragments of Saxon crosses and tombstones which probably pre-date the establishment of the see.

Despite its endowments Ramsbury was considered a poor bishopric, especially by its last incumbent, Bishop Herman. Herman may be considered the architect of the medieval diocese of Salisbury, because, having failed to persuade the king to move his seat to Malmesbury, it was upon his insistence (motivated, it appears by greed) that the sees of Sherborne and Ramsbury were combined in 1058. This brought Dorset, Wiltshire and Berkshire together in a single diocese, based first at Sherborne, but after the Norman conquest at Old Sarum. The rearrangement and subsequent move should be set against a general restlessness among bishops of the period. In the space of about forty years, 1050-1090, five other sees moved from what were

The footings of the forsaken Old Sarum Cathedral, as revealed by archaeological excavation before the First World War.

considered inappropriately rural locations to more populous towns, such as Exeter, Chester and Norwich.

But was Old Sarum a populous town when Bishop Herman arrived there from Sherborne in 1075? Probably not, although it had the potential for being one, and the Norman government seemed to be encouraging it to grow at the gates of its impressive new castle, as Devizes would do a generation later. A new cathedral on a virgin site, its architecture and clerical organization derived from Norman models, was also an exciting prospect – but not perhaps for Herman, who had by now become rather long in the tooth. He died in 1078, and it was left to his successor, Osmund, to be the innovator.

The footings of Old Sarum Cathedral, uncovered for all to see by archaeologists working between 1912 and 1914, give only a faint impression of the way the building might have looked, and convey nothing of the two remarkable men, Bishops Osmund (1078-99) and Roger (1102-39), who were largely responsible for it. Osmund's cathedral, which was consecrated in 1092 and promptly damaged by a thunderstorm, was small, with transeptal towers (as at Exeter) and a squat presbytery ending in an apse. Roger rebuilt the east end and transepts on a grander scale, but died in disfavour before he could set to work on Osmund's nave.

Neither man, however, is principally remembered for his work on the cathedral fabric. Osmund's lasting achievement lay

The tomb of Bishop Roger, now in Salisbury Cathedral. A powerful twelfth-century statesman, Roger controlled both castle and cathedral at Old Sarum, and encompassed the latter wihin the walls of the former.

in setting out in a written constitution the ground rules for organizing the chapter in a medieval cathedral. His rules commanded great respect and were widely copied elsewhere. Roger was essentially a doughty politician and government administrator. Although he spent lavishly on Old Sarum, his decision to extend the curtain wall of his castle around the cathedral, thus embracing the one within the other, was ultimately to lead to the cathedral's abandonment a century later. It was Osmund, later *Saint* Osmund, who was remembered with affection and awe at Salisbury, not Roger.

The often-told tale, of privation and harassment at Old Sarum, of the bishop's vision of a new cathedral in the fecund meadows, and of the drift of the population down into the foursquare city, as it sprang up all around the bustling building site, is too well known to bear repeating here. It is sufficient to say that between 1220, when the foundation stones were laid, and about 1266, when work ceased, one of the supreme accomplishments of medieval architecture came to grace the south Wiltshire landscape. Around the cathedral were grouped the canons' houses in their close, and beyond lay the city, destined to become one of the largest and most important in medieval England.

Salisbury Cathedral, with its shafts of contrasting light and dark limestones, its trios of clean-lined lancet windows, and above all its unity of Early English composition, is justly famous around the world. The spire, which is later than the rest, but by less than a century, is the tallest medieval survivor in England. The close, distinguished by the elegance of its town houses of many centuries, is indubitably the finest anywhere. The constitutions of its chapter, and the cycle of its ceremonies (the 'Use of Sarum') were adopted throughout the province of Canterbury, and elsewhere. The shrine of St Osmund, both before and after he was canonized in 1457, became a magnet for pilgrims.

But, leaving aside the superlatives, how did the existence of the cathedral actually affect the clergy and laity dotted around the Wiltshire countryside? At one level, as the nub of religious life in the county, its officers supervised the work and worship of the local church. Priests had to be ordained, and instituted to their livings by the bishop. If they wished to be absent from their cure

The grandeur of Salisbury Cathedral choir, looking east to the chancel and Trinity Chapel. The painted ceiling roundels and the strainer arches strengthening the crossing of the eastern transepts are clearly seen.

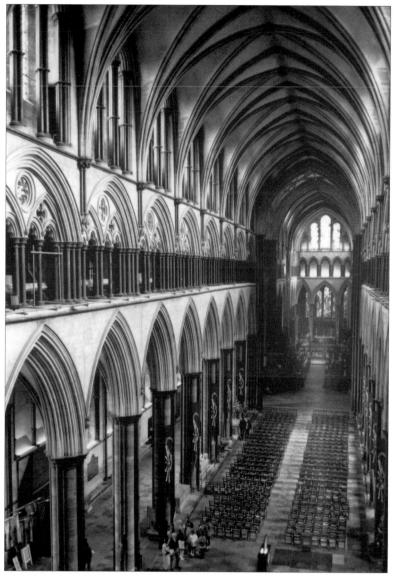

One of the most spectacular views of the cathedral interior is gained by standing in front of the west window at triforium level.

for a period, to study perhaps or to undertake a pilgrimage, they needed the bishop's licence, and he must be satisfied that adequate provision would be made in their absence. If unorthodox theology was being promulgated the culprits must be made to conform, or be excommunicated. If the rector or parishioners wished to extend their church, or modify the fabric in any way, the bishop's permission had to be sought, and he had to consecrate the new work. Periodically he, his two archdeacons, or for certain parishes the dean, went on a tour of inspection, known as a visitation, and then defects of all kinds might be revealed. For instance, when the dean visited the chapels dependent on Calne in May 1409, he was interested not only in the broken window in Cherhill chancel, and that sheep were fouling the porch, but also in the absence of a parish clerk for Calstone and Quemerford, and the failure of the vicar of Calne to perform the burial service properly. Furthermore he arbitrated in cases of perjury, defamation and a dispute over tithe payments, and he passed judgement on various sexual offenders, including a deacon alleged to have fornicated with a stranger in Calne church.

Medieval bishops were tireless travellers, peregrinating around their dioceses, and making frequent official visits to London and occasional trips abroad. On their larger manors they had substantial houses, where with their retinues they could transact business, and sojourn for periods. Thomas Langton, who was Bishop of Salisbury from 1485 to 1493, spent much of his episcopate when not on the road at Woodford, Ramsbury, Sonning (in Berkshire), Sherborne, or London. Other episcopal centres were Chardstock in Dorset, Potterne, and of course the Bishop's Palace in Salisbury.

Among Langton's concerns was the growing number of rebellious voices raised against the clergy and doctrines of mother church. In 1491 Richard Lyllingston of Castle Combe was reported for expressing the wish, 'that all the Churches within all Cristendome wer in the myddys of helle,' and for ridiculing and intimidating preachers by contradicting their sermons in the alehouse. As punishment for such defiance the bishop's consistory court at Salisbury, under the presidency of the chancellor, imposed a penance designed to humiliate him. He was to be led, wearing shirt and breeches, with a bundle of faggots on his back and bearing a stick in his right

The Bishop's Palace in the Close, seen from the cathedral tower. It is now home to the Cathedral School.

hand, round various places — Salisbury market place, the cathedral, Cricklade market place and church, Malmesbury, Castle Combe and Chippenham, confessing in each place the error of his ways.

A similarly elaborate penalty was meted out by Bishop Hallum eighty years earlier from his manor house at Potterne upon five malefactors for forcibly removing a man who had taken sanctuary in Grittleton church. They must prostrate themselves at the cathedral west door, dressed only in linen shirts, while the dean said over them the psalm, 'Have mercy on me, O Lord'. If they showed contrition they might then enter the cathedral, genuflect at the font, and offer a twopenny candle each at the step of the high altar. Such colourful punishments take their place in the bishops' registers alongside reports on dilapidations, disputes over tithes, institutions and consecrations, and other kinds of miscellaneous business.

In all these respects the cathedral spire cast its pointing shadow over the whole diocese. But a considerable number of parishes had a more onerous link with what went on in Salisbury Close. These were the places which paid for much of it. The running of the cathedral was financed in various ways. The bishop himself was a major landowner, with manors scattered across the diocese and beyond. In north Wiltshire he owned Ramsbury with two adjoining manors, Bishopstone and Baydon; in the centre of the county were the large estates of Bishop's Cannings, Potterne (which included Worton and Marston), and West Lavington; and in the south was the bishop's city of Salisbury itself, together with nearby Milford and Woodford. The dean and chapter, too, built up a large portfolio, not only of land, but also of tithes derived from churches which they had appropriated. The income went into a pot known as the common fund, from which the canons drew a stipend. But other income from tithes was specific to individual canons or functionaries, through the system of prebends.

A prebend was a form of appropriation, the process whereby the tithes accruing from a parish were diverted from their original purpose, which was the maintenance of religious services, personnel and buildings within that parish, to some other function. We saw in chapter two how the medieval parish church was regarded in some sense as a business, operated under franchise from the bishop and the central church authorities. The advowson, or right to nominate the rector (who was the beneficiary of the profits from that business) could be sold or bequeathed, and very many churches (at least 113 in Wiltshire, as we have noted) passed by this means into the hands of religious houses and cathedral clergy. They received the tithes, and employed a priest to be their substitute (which is the literal meaning of 'vicar') in the parish. He was paid a stipend, or a proportion of the tithe income. When the monasteries were dissolved at the reformation these appropriated rectories were purchased along with other monastic property by laymen, who became known as 'lay rectors', and their parishes continued to be vicarages. This explains, at the simplest level, why the incumbents of some churches are rectors, while others are served by vicars.

The benefices of churches appropriated to canons of the cathedral chapter were known as prebends, and the canons were prebendaries, who took their titles from the parishes which supported them. Of the eventual total of 52 or 53 it has been suggested that about 28 prebends can be traced back to the original endowment of the chapter when it was established by Osmund at Old Sarum. They were mostly created from benefices within the diocese which had belonged to Osmund himself as bishop, for example on estates which he owned, but a few derived their income from land, offerings at cathedral altars, or churches outside the diocese, including Grantham in far-off Lincolnshire. Gifts of further benefices and land flooded into the chapter during the twelfth century and later, donated by kings and laymen, as well as by bishops and others. In this way the profits of large Wiltshire parishes such as Calne and Westbury went to support the treasurer and precentor respectively, while Highworth, Netheravon, Burbage and several other places gave their name to prebends. Parishes thus appropriated to members of the chapter also fell under different administrative procedures, and were known as peculiars.

Although prebendaries were usually associated with cathedrals, a few of the great nunneries also had prebends attached to them, in order to pay for priests to say mass and officiate for the nuns. Wilton Abbey was one of these. It owned the lucrative prebend of Chalke in the Ebble Valley, and several others, including North Newnton in Pewsey Vale. This prebend, with its distant chapelry at West Knoyle, near Mere, was held at the dissolution as a sinecure by the famous traveller John Leland, who appears to have visited both places during his last itinerary, perhaps in 1545.

Wilton Abbey, like the other great Wiltshire religious houses, was a major landowner, and its possessions included a number of advowsons and appropriated churches. A common route whereby a piece of land or the advowson of a parish church came into the hands of a monastic community was as a bequest by a landowner, in return for prayers for his soul, or for the privilege of burial in the monastery's church. Bradenstoke Priory, for example, which stood next to what is now the perimeter of Lyneham airfield, received much of its estate in the form of grants by Earls of Salisbury and members of their family. It had in fact been founded in 1139 by the father of

The architecture of the prebendal church of Calne now reflects the late medieval prosperity of its town. But it was the centre of a large and important estate much earlier, when it supported Edmund, the treasurer who masterminded the fundraising for Salisbury Cathedral. Edmund went on to become archbishop of Canterbury, and was later canonized as St Edmund of Abingdon.

the first earl, so this family allegiance is not surprising. When in about 1190 the priory's possessions were confirmed by the bishop, they included the church at Bradenstoke, the chapel at Lake, and land at Etchilhampton, from the founder; the manor and church at Wilcot from the first earl; and a chapel at Chitterne and a church in Dorset from the second. There were many other gifts and bequests from landowners. Philip Basset, for example, gave to the Bradenstoke canons land, a house, and

the advowson of the church at Marden in Pewsey Vale, for the
souls of his wife and his brother, a former Bishop of London.
Henry de la Mare gave his tenement at Winterbourne Earls near
Salisbury to the church at Bradenstoke, 'in which he has vowed
to be buried', for his salvation and that of his wife. When a
widow named Constance inherited land at Fisherton Delamare
in the Wylye Valley on her father's death, she touchingly gave a
portion of it to the canons, 'for the soul of Godfrey of St
Martin, her husband, now at rest in the church of Bradenstoke'.

The influence of the monasteries, both as landowners on
the agriculture and economy of medieval Wiltshire, and as
rectors and patrons on the fabric of its churches, was immense.
Even a relatively small and poor abbey, such as Wiltshire's only
Cistercian house, at Stanley near Calne, built up a large holding
of estates scattered throughout the west country, operated one
of the earliest known fulling mills, and participated not only in
the export trade of wool to Italy, but also owned quarries of
Bath stone and had the right to extract iron ore for smelting
from Pewsham Forest.

Wherever you went in medieval Wiltshire you would have
found land which was farmed, either directly or leased to
tenants, by religious houses. The three great Wiltshire
communities, Malmesbury, Wilton, and Amesbury, all had
substantial holdings within the county, as did many of the lesser
houses. And they jostled with interests from further afield, such
as the powerful abbeys of Glastonbury, Shaftesbury and
Winchester. Impressive barns survive on two of Shaftesbury's

A fragment of monastic
architecture surviving from a
sixteenth-century outbuilding of the
vanished Stanley Abbey.

Wiltshire estates, Bradford on Avon and Tisbury, and these would have been used to store the produce of the abbey's farms pending cartage to market or to Shaftesbury. In 1367, for example, one-third of the wheat produced at Bradford was taken to Shaftesbury, and virtually all the malted barley. This was transported in five convoys, using carts not only from Bradford, but also from other abbey manors, at Donhead, Tisbury and Sedgehill.

As rectors of parish churches some monasteries were more conscientious than others in maintaining and improving the fabric. Amesbury was refounded as a priory in 1177, and as part of its new endowment it received four nearby rectories, at Amesbury, Bulford, Durrington and Maddington. But a recent

Place Barn, Tisbury. The massive produce barn of Shaftesbury Abbey's large and lucrative manor of Tisbury, was still used until recently for storing grain.

The twelfth-century rebuilding of Chirton church seems to have taken place as a consequence of its appropriation by Lanthony Priory, Gloucester. The fine roof timbers from this refurbishment are still in place.

study concludes that these churches share no distinctive feature, and that when Durrington and Maddington chancels were rebuilt during the thirteenth century it was in a simple fashion. By contrast in Pewsey Vale two neighbouring churches seem to have had substantial sums lavished on them by their monastic owners. At Chirton the rectory was appropriated by Lanthony Priory, Gloucester, in 1167, and its south doorway, nave arcades, splendid roof and font all seem to date from about this period. At Urchfont the sumptuous vaulted chancel must have been paid for by St Mary's Nunnery, Winchester, who held the living as a prebend. It has been suggested that the rebuilding was in response to a criticism made about the poor state of the chancel during the Bishop of Salisbury's visitation in 1301.

No detailed discussion of the histories of all the monasteries, friaries, religious hospitals and colleges which existed in medieval Wiltshire can be attempted in this book. As we have already noted, there were nearly fifty of them – about twenty monasteries, nunneries and friaries; another twenty hospitals; and about ten monastic cells, granges and secular colleges. Considerable uncertainty surrounds some of them and, with a few notable exceptions, little of their fabric survives. Even the sites of some of the more obscure are unknown. Among the more important monasteries the houses at Kington St Michael and Monkton Farleigh in west Wiltshire, Bradenstoke near Lyneham, and Ivychurch near Salisbury are all represented now only by fragments. Stanley Abbey, the Cistercian house in its peaceful valley near Calne, has gone, but earthworks on the site reveal something of its layout, and a nearby farmhouse and outbuildings were probably associated with it. Easton, near Burbage, has a rare Elizabethan church (drastically restored in the nineteenth century) which may

Ivychurch Priory, on the edge of Clarendon Park near Salisbury, is one of several Wiltshire monasteries to survive only as fragments. This free-standing pier fronts a farmhouse which incorporates medieval features.

occupy the site of a friary church damaged by fire in 1493. At Maiden Bradley, close to the Somerset border, a late-medieval building survives which is believed to have been connected with the priory and leper hospital there. One of the two Wiltshire preceptories, or monasteries of orders of knights, was established at Ansty, near Tisbury (the other, referred to earlier, was at Temple Rockley), and a building thought to have been its guesthouse remains.

Several Wiltshire monasteries and nunneries were adapted or destroyed at the dissolution to make way for mansion houses. Longleat was a poor priory which has disappeared beneath a

In a tranquil south Wiltshire setting near Tisbury this medieval building at Ansty is believed to be the hospice of a preceptory, which the Knights Hospitallers established in the village.

rich mansion, whereas at Wilton a rich nunnery was replaced by an equally rich mansion. The small grange of a French monastery at Avebury seems to have been on the site of the present Avebury Manor. Nothing remains to be seen of these three, but at Amesbury and Lacock the story is rather different.

Amesbury, like Malmesbury and Wilton, traced its foundation back to before the Norman conquest, but it was refounded in 1177, as we have already noted. The new church and conventual buildings, for nuns of the French order of Font Evrault, were probably built on a different site, some 300 metres from their predecessor, which was a smaller Benedictine nunnery.

Amesbury parish church probably served as the church of the first nunnery and, after this nunnery was refounded on a nearby site in 1177, the church was rebuilt and continued to be used by the male religious as well as the parish.

Left: The fine late-medieval vaulted cloister of Lacock Abbey formed the nucleus of the mansion which was built on the abbey site after the Dissolution.

Opposite: Part of the *tour de force* of Norman sculpture in the porch of Malmesbury Abbey. Six apostles sit beneath a flying angel, facing their six counterparts across the porch.

Of the Fontevraldine house nothing remains, and the site is now occupied by the mansion house known as Amesbury Abbey. But the fine parish church is believed to have belonged originally to the first abbey, having survived and been rebuilt after 1177 as the church of the lay brethren and male religious employed by the nunnery, as well as serving the townspeople of Amesbury.

At Lacock, which was also taken over at the dissolution to become a mansion, the abbey church has disappeared, but many of the conventual buildings, including the beautiful vaulted cloister, have survived, incorporated into the later house. Like Amesbury it was a house for women, in this case Augustinian canonesses (although the founder's original idea may have been a Cistercian nunnery), and it was established even later than the refounded Amesbury, in 1232. Another similarity between Lacock and Amesbury (and apparent also at Bradenstoke) was the

way in which the religious houses stimulated trade in the communities at their gates. In each place a modest market place was laid out and the topography of the settlement altered.

Only the two most notable examples of monastic church architecture surviving in Wiltshire, at Malmesbury and Edington, remain to be mentioned. Malmesbury, the most important religious site in the county, has preserved most of the nave, the south porch, and fragments of the crossing of its cathedral-like abbey church. The breathtaking south porch has been described as, 'among the best pieces of Norman sculpture and decoration in England'. Once inside, the visitor is confronted by the magnificent twelfth-century transitional Norman arcades supporting a fourteenth-century lierne vault. But the scheme comes to an abrupt end with the blank east wall, where once stood the crossing, central tower, and soaring spire. The nave has survived because it was taken over by the townspeople as their parish church at the dissolution. Of the former parish church, St Paul's, only the tower and spire remain, at the corner of the abbey churchyard.

Edington, which shelters beneath the northern escarpment of Salisbury Plain near Westbury, was one of only two monastic houses of an order similar to Augustinian canons, known as Bonshommes. It was founded in 1358 by a native of the village who became Bishop of Winchester and a leading politician; probably it was his connection with Edward the Black Prince, patron of the Bonshommes' other house, which influenced his decision to establish them at Edington. The

Opposite: The imposing Norman north arcade of Malmesbury Abbey ends abruptly with a solid wall where the crossing should be. Only the nave was retained for parish worship.

conventual buildings have disappeared, but the marvellous church remains, long and battlemented against the backdrop of the hillside, and a perfect illustration of the way in which the Decorated style of the fourteenth century was metamorphosed into the Perpendicular of the fifteenth.

When Chaucer's Wife of Bath travelled through Wiltshire, we imagine, in the 1390s, Edington was still almost new, and its brethren (for they did not call themselves monks) were singing daily in their church. Now, six centuries later, a summer week each year is set apart here for a festival of liturgical music, and then one can still experience the serenity of plainsong, as through the traceried windows the downland hillside darkens against the evening sky. It is time for us to turn to medieval religion, as glimpsed in the architecture and decoration of Wiltshire's churches.

Images of Belief

I SUPPOSE that most of us, if taken to some remote spot – the Amazonian jungle, perhaps, or the mountains of Nepal – and shown a building which we were told was a temple, would try to work out from its design, its furnishings and its imagery just what was the nature of the religion which it served. Prehistorians interpreting the 'ritual' monuments of European antiquity have to resort to the same process of deduction. But when we visit an English parish church we tend to assume that it was built to contain the kind of religious observance which is still practised there, and with which most of us have at least a nodding acquaintance. A moment's reflection, of course, will tell us that this is a false assumption, and in this chapter we shall try to piece together some fragments of medieval religion, as displayed in Wiltshire churches.

A shaft of sunlight is directed on to the altar of St Laurence's Church, Bradford on Avon, from a carefully positioned Saxon window.

First we need to strip away the accretions which have arrived since the reformation. These will include many of the internal furnishings, as well as the structural repairs and alterations carried out by Victorian restorers. They are considered in later chapters. And along with all this paraphernalia we should set on one side the Anglican liturgy which we have come to associate with it. Then, drawing upon the fragmentary evidence of surviving wall-paintings, sculpture, fixtures and fittings, we should try to reconstruct the appearance of the medieval interior. This we must place alongside the written evidence of church life, as described in churchwardens' accounts, diocesan records, and the works of theological authors.

Immediately we discover that the nature of medieval worship was not static; it evolved and developed through the centuries. This is evident from the architectural history of most churches. We saw in chapter two how a series of building phases can usually be detected, a 'nest' or 'stack' of churches, interrelating and interlocking on the same site. Not all of these modifications can be explained by technical advances in the construction industry, the need for extra accommodation, or routine repair of dilapidated fabric. Why, for example, was the chancel lengthened and new windows inserted, why was an elaborate side chapel added or a new porch built, why was money spent on pews and a pulpit as the middle ages drew to a close? The obvious explanation is that such changes were tailored to the requirements of an evolving pattern of worship and belief.

At Bradford on Avon we can see, side by side, the beginning and end of this evolutionary process. Inside the late-Saxon church of St Laurence there is an aura of intense mystery, and to submit to its darkness by entering on a sunny day can be a profoundly awesome experience. In the morning a small window bathes the tall, narrow chancel arch in light, and through it we glimpse another shaft, thrown like a spotlight from a second window, which directs our eye on to the altar. At Breamore, close to Downton (but in Hampshire), a similar Saxon arch is inscribed with words which mean 'Here the word is revealed unto you', and much the same sentiment was presumably intended by the Bradford architect's use of light and shade. But crossing the road, we find that a very different building presents itself. Here the parish church of the Holy Trinity has evolved from Norman (and probably Saxon) phases. Its Norman chancel was extended eastward in about 1300, and the simple round-headed windows were augmented by a large five-light east window. The chancel walls were adorned with paintings, two recesses were made for tombs, and an elaborate piscina – for washing the communion vessels – was installed. Later, the wealthy clothiers of Bradford paid to refurbish the nave in Perpendicular style, and build a tower, north aisle, south chapel and south porch. In the aisle and chapel they installed altars and made themselves chantries, and in the nave they provided a new font. Light streamed through the new windows, and illuminated the murals, the finely-shafted piers, the painted screen, and the inscriptions on the brasses. Here was a religion awesome in its affluence – but the element of mystery had gone.

The use of light, with its obvious Biblical metaphor, is only one example of changing fashions in religion. Others might be the scope that aisles offered for solemn and impressive processions within the church; or the late-medieval predilection for towers, which had absolutely no effect on the devotions of those within, but made a statement to the world outside about the church's importance and grandeur. But of particular significance to the congregation must have been those parts of the church where their 'rites of passage' were administered: the font where at birth they were admitted to the Christian community; the porch where they were married (only after the marriage had been performed did the couple enter the church to celebrate the nuptial mass); and the churchyard (or if they were wealthy enough, the tomb within the church) where they would be buried.

Opposite: The huge font of Tournai marble which seems to have been rescued for Preshute church from Marlborough Castle, which lay within its parish.

Eight named virtues vanquish the corresponding vices around the Norman font at Stanton Fitzwarren.

Below: The Norman font at Avebury. A bishop (his head defaced by a staple for the font cover) triumphs over two serpents, which come at him from both directions.

The rite of baptism, during which the new-born child was exorcised of the evil forces surrounding it, imbued the font with a particular status within the church. Instances, such as at Bradford, of its replacement when the church was rebuilt, are quite rare. More commonly the original font was retained, and now is often the oldest portion of the building to survive. In chapter one we admired the Saxon font at Potterne, which stands in the thirteenth-century church. There are more than fifty Norman fonts in Wiltshire churches, reflecting no doubt the time that those churches were first permanently built in stone or achieved parochial status. Preshute church, next to Marlborough, has one of the largest and finest medieval fonts in Wiltshire. It is made of black marble from Tournai in France, and is believed to have come from the royal chapel within Marlborough Castle. But when the parishioners of Preshute acquired this notable ornament (perhaps in the fifteenth century) they were loth to abandon the earlier font in which they had all been baptized, and which was probably contemporary with the building of their Norman church. They kept it, and now it can be seen built into the porch.

Fonts, too, because they held in thrall the powers of darkness, were suitable objects for symbolic decoration. Stanton Fitzwarren, near Highworth, possesses a remarkably fine font, which displays the personified virtues standing triumphantly on their corresponding vices. At Westwood a grimacing devil (known as 'the Old Lad of Westwood') looks down on the font from above, formerly with the inscription, 'Resist me and I will

The annunciation, depicted on the font at Upavon. The lily in the pot between the two figures symbolizes Mary.

flee'. Avebury's Norman font is a cauldron veritably seething with Christian power, on which a heroic bishop skewers a gasping serpent with his crozier. At Upavon the font depicts a less turbulent scene – the annunciation, with the standing figures of Mary and the angel, the holy dove descending, and Mary's symbol, the lily in a jar.

At the other end of life the belief that repeated prayers would help to ensure the soul's passage into a blissful eternity was a powerful incentive to men and women of means to support churches, monasteries and other religious foundations. In the later middle ages they spent lavishly on their parish churches, by providing sumptuous chapels in which prayers were to be said for their salvation, day in, day out, from the time of their death until the final judgement. The north aisle at

Bradford is formed out of two such chantry chapels, with altars dedicated to St Nicholas and Our Lady. They were endowed in 1420 and 1524, and on the same day in 1524 a third chantry, at the principal altar in the chancel, was created by the vicar.

The most impressive chantry in a Wiltshire village church is the Baynton chapel at Bromham near Devizes. Although it now takes its name from the family whose private chapel it became after the reformation, it was built in 1492, or a few

The spectacular chantry of the late fifteenth century at Bromham, known as the Baynton Chapel.

The chantry of the Giffard family, with its memorable circular window, was established in 1279 at Boyton in the Wylye Valley.

years earlier, to commemorate Elizabeth Beauchamp, together with her two husbands and their families. Other lavish chapels in out-of-the-way places are the Giffard chantry at Boyton in the Wylye valley, established in 1279, and the Borbach chantry, all that remains of the old parish church of West Dean, on the border with Hampshire. Of town churches with chantries there is a spectacular example at Mere, the fourteenth-century Bettesthorne chapel. This is the finer of two chapels, north and south of the chancel, and it contains a brass to the memory of Sir John Bettesthorne, its founder, who died in 1398. Both chapels have good late-medieval wooden screens.

The logistics of storing up an uninterrupted supply of efficacious prayers involved not only providing a chapel, but also staffing it with a chaplain or chantry priest, and in many cases building him somewhere to live — a chantry house. Founding a chantry was an expensive business, therefore, and beyond the pockets of ordinary parishioners, who nevertheless might feel that their souls too after death would need the intercession that chantry prayers supplied. For such people a 'group membership' was the only expedient. At St Thomas's Church, Salisbury, for instance, the well-known south chapel paid for by William Swayne to house a chantry on behalf of his family, also came to be the guild chapel of the Tailors, to which he belonged. Other guild members, in return for a small bequest or donation, might have their names entered on a list known as a bede-roll, to be duly prayed for after death by their surviving fellow tailors and by the priest.

Such an arrangement was of considerable antiquity, and Wiltshire furnishes one of the earliest pieces of evidence for it. A copy of the gospels once in use at Great Bedwyn (and now in Switzerland) contains tenth-century notes about a local guild. Its rules begin, 'If any member meet his death, let everyone have five masses or five psalters said for the dead man's soul'. Other instructions include payments to the mass-priest (who was presumably one of the secular priests attached to Bedwyn's minster), and a regular penny subscription collected from members at guild meetings, 'for their souls'. But it was in the later middle ages that guilds in towns assumed far greater importance, not only as social clubs, but also as agents of local government and chambers of trade. Bound up with these responsibilities continued the urge to worship together, take part in religious processions on saint's days (hence the Salisbury Tailors' famous processional giant), and commemorate deceased members in their prayers. At Devizes, for example, the emerging borough corporation in 1392 authorized its mayor to create a chantry to support a priest at an altar in St John's Church. It was to be for the benefit of the king and queen, other royalty, and the mayor and commons, and their kindred.

From these examples it is clear that the chantry system extended beyond the mere repeating of prayers in church, into the social fabric of medieval life. It also had two other more religious implications. On the one hand it greatly increased the number of clergy living and working within parishes, and these men, like curates nowadays, could play an important role in the welfare of the community, assisting the parish priest and perhaps teaching pupils the rudiments of religious education. When a tax on clergy was imposed in 1379 it was found that, in addition to the rector, there were at St Thomas's Church, Salisbury, twenty-one chaplains. At St Edmund's there were a further eighteen. A roll call in 1432 listed 57 clergymen then attached to St Thomas's in various capacities. In consequence, when the chantry system was abolished in 1548, parishes complained about the consequent loss of manpower. At Malmesbury, for instance, the parishioners petitioned the king for assistant clergy to replace the chantry priests who had formerly served them.

The other religious implication of chantry-like beliefs was that some of the more elaborate foundations included not only provision for prayers said in a chapel, but also money given for some other pious or charitable purpose. The monastery at Edington, for example, grew out of William of Edington's original intention merely to found a chantry in his native parish church. The Hungerford family's foundation at Heytesbury (which still exists) was founded as a hospital with a warden, twelve poor men and one poor woman, drawn in preference from among the family's workforce. The warden's duties included administering the hospital, conducting services there and in the parish church, and teaching Heytesbury children grammar, as well as saying prayers for members of the Hungerford family and their retainers. Another of the eighteen foundations in medieval Wiltshire recorded as hospitals ('almshouses' would be the modern expression for most of them) was a community of thirteen poor men (or men and women) at Wilton known as 'Magdalens'. They lived in the Hospital of St Mary Magdalene, and were supported by the nuns of Wilton Abbey. Their function was to pray for the soul of St Edith, the

Fine carved pulpit in the Salisbury joiners' tradition, at Bishopstone in the Ebble valley. Notice the devilish creatures climbing along its top.

patron saint of the abbey. Not all the medieval hospitals had so direct a connection with the chantry system, but most originated from deathbed piety, in the same way as the landed wealth of the monasteries which we observed in chapter three.

From this excursion into the side chapels of the medieval church we should now return to the nave. Until the late fifteenth century we shall find no seating for the congregation, who were expected to stand or kneel during services. Only the weak, elderly and infirm might be allowed to 'go to the wall', where in some cases (such as at Bratton) a stone ledge or seat was provided. Very occasionally in parish churches misericords (the word means 'mercy') were provided in the choir stalls, against which clergy could lean while still appearing to stand; in Wiltshire (apart from the cathedral) they are found only at Edington, Highworth, Mere and St Thomas's, Salisbury. The appearance of fixed wooden seating in many churches during the last century of the middle ages coincided with the installation of pulpits and lecterns, and no great power of deduction is needed to see that they were linked. The late medieval church placed increasing emphasis on reading and expounding the Christian message, and this placed an extra demand on the stamina of the congregation.

One of the carved bench-ends in Crudwell church, which are mentioned by John Aubrey.

In some parts of England the emergence of pews was accompanied by a blossoming of imaginative and sometimes ribald woodcarving. The bench ends of Devon, Cornwall and Somerset are well-known. But in Wiltshire no similar tradition seems to have developed, and we have little to show for it. However, we may concur with John Aubrey's opinion, who, when writing about Crudwell (near Malmesbury) said that, 'here are the best and most substantial seats that I know anywhere'. He added that they were made by a certain Walton, whose rebus was carved on one. A rebus is a kind of punning logo, and indeed one carving had the letters WAL above a barrel, or 'tun' (it has since disappeared). Others have human heads, a stag and a Tudor rose. There are bench ends too at

Britford and Durnford, and fine carved pulpits of this period at Potterne and West Kington, near Castle Combe. The best medieval lectern in Wiltshire is at St Martin's Church, Salisbury, a brass eagle with the expression of a true aristocrat among birds.

The late-medieval eagle lectern at St Martin's Church, Salisbury.

As with chantries, so the pewing of churches had wider implications. The system of paying rent for a particular pew brought revenue to the church, but fragmented the congregation, as we shall see in the next chapter. A more immediate effect was that the variety of uses to which church naves could be put was drastically curtailed. A major source of income for parish churches throughout the middle ages, and until the puritan onslaught of the seventeenth century, was the holding of ales, or drinking-feasts, for various purposes. Such village parties might be convened to commemorate some particular event, such as a wedding; or they would be regular annual affairs, often associated with the patronal festival or saint's day of the church dedication. Dancing of a semi-religious or apparently pagan nature might take place as part of the entertainments. Despite episcopal condemnations dating back in Salisbury diocese to the thirteenth century, ales were clearly too popular and remunerative to be abandoned, and there is occasional evidence that they were held, if not in the church itself, then certainly in the churchyard. A reference in the churchwardens' accounts of St Edmund's, Salisbury, for example, in 1490 includes a payment for cleaning the church after the 'Dawnse of Powles', or *danse macabre* had taken place there. At Mere the principal income derived by the churchwardens continued to be the church ale well into Elizabeth's reign, and the celebrations (no longer, if ever, held within the church, as it by now had seats) included something akin to a modern carnival queen. In 1567, for example, we find a note in the accounts: 'John Watts the sonne of Thomas Watts is appointed to be Cuckowe King this next yeare according to the old order, because hee was Prince the last yeare. . . And because John Watts hath ben long sick hit is agreed that if hee be not able to srve at the tyme of the Church ale. That then John Coward... shall srve and be king in his place for this yeare.'

Dancing and feasting were not the only activities to be held in and around the church. The king in 1246 granted a four-day fair to be held around St Peter's churchyard in Marlborough, in connection with the saint's feast, and St Edmund's, Salisbury, in 1490 was taking a toll from cheese-dealers who had their pitches against the church wall. There is even a reference to a horsefair being held in Salisbury Cathedral!

Partly in response to the new limitations placed upon activities within church, many parishes built for themselves the equivalent of village halls, which were known as church houses. In the rambling preface to his essay on north Wiltshire, dated 1670, John Aubrey recalled (through rose-tinted spectacles) that as late as his grandfather's day there were no poor rates in Kington St Michael: 'the Church Ale at Whitsuntide did their businesse. In every Parish is, or was, a church howse, to which belonged spitts, crocks, etc, utensils for dressing provision. Here the Howsekeepers met, and were merry and gave their Charitie: the young people came there too, and had dancing, bowling, shooting at buttes, etc, the ancients sitting gravely by, looking on. All things were civill and without scandall.' At Mere in the 1560s, when we hear of the cuckoo king, they did not have a church house, but they seem to have been saving up for one, as several parishioners left money in their wills towards the cost. It is said to have been built eventually in about 1580, and survived in a dilapidated state until 1890. Among several church houses remaining in Wiltshire there is a fine example at Bradford on Avon, and another at Sherston, which was rebuilt after the little town's disastrous fire in 1511. The contract for rebuilding it has survived, and we know that it cost £10.

But we have been seduced away from church again, and must enter once more. Inside, we are often told, the medieval church was a riot of symbolism and colour – rich carvings, intricate sculpture, painted walls, painted glass, painted panels. This should not surprise us, for in a world in which literacy and books were uncommon, and religion was conducted in an alien language, the information had to be conveyed by visual images. And although only a tiny fraction has survived, its message is straightforward enough. Medieval Christianity was a struggle between the opposing forces of good and evil, light and darkness, Christ and the Devil. In the end good will prevail, but meanwhile in this world (epitomized by the parish church) the battle would rage. Thus the imagery within the church depicted, on the one hand, the forces of good – Christ crucified, his mother Mary, the saints and apostles, the characters of the Bible story – and on the other hand the forces of evil – devils and serpents, and the whole pagan pantheon which lurked in the medieval subconscious. The Devil was no less real than the saints, and his place too was in the church, for without him and his tribe the cosmic struggle could not be played out there each Sunday.

Between them, the churches of Wiltshire display a rich heritage of medieval imagery, with most of the leading *dramatis personae* somewhere to be found. Christ crucified and Christ in majesty naturally figure as the focus of devotions, and were generally to be found at the centre of the church, the chancel

This grinning Norman corbel was once on an exterior wall of St John's Church, Devizes, but since the fifteenth century has been protected by the roof of the Beauchamp Chapel.

arch. The rood, or image of Christ on the cross, was elevated above a screen across the arch. To give access to it a walkway known as a rood loft ran along the top of the screen, and access to it was generally gained by a staircase within the thickness of the wall. The doors to the rood stair are frequently seen, although the roods and rood screens themselves were usually destroyed at the reformation. The Saxon angels now high above the chancel arch in St Laurence's Chapel, Bradford, are believed to have formed part of a rood, and at Durnford a much-decayed wall painting around the arch may have served as the backcloth to a rood. The best surviving screens in their original positions are at Avebury and Mere, the latter with a Victorian loft and rood above. Others include the reused screen at Compton Bassett, a restored screen at Edington, and several

Three examples of medieval figurative sculpture. From left: Christ triumphs over a dragon at Stanton St Quintin; St John Baptist at Colerne; 'Rattlebone' at Sherston. Although probably a monk holding a book, local legend has long identified this figure with the legendary Rattlebone who, though mortally wounded, fought on to defend Sherston while holding a tile to his injured stomach.

which have been removed to subsidiary places in their churches.

An alternative centrepiece was a doom, or representation of the day of judgement painted on the spandrels of the chancel arch. The doom in St Thomas's Church, Salisbury, painted over at the reformation, and discovered and restored in the nineteenth-century, is justly famous. It is the work of a sophisticated late-medieval artist, and incorporates a feast of

Few rood screens and lofts survived the Reformation, but Avebury boasts an excellent late-medieval example.

One of the flying angels now built high into the wall above the chancel arch in St Laurence's Saxon church, Bradford-on-Avon. They were probably once part of a rood.

imagery eloquent of the medieval hope of resurrection. Here sits Christ in majesty, his feet on the world, flanked by the instuments of his passion; beneath him the apostles lined up as a tribunal, and around him the celestial city. Corpses are escorted from their graves by angels blowing trumpets, and some are led into the gates of heaven; others are ushered past a taunting devil into the jaws of a dreadful gaping monster. But no verbal description can do it justice. It is a visual statement, and is best appreciated with binoculars.

Fragments of wall paintings survive in many Wiltshire churches, while in others, such as Winterbourne Dauntsey, near Salisbury, a photographic record was made before they were destroyed in the nineteenth century. The most interesting series is at Purton, where a variety of scenes is depicted on Biblical themes and from medieval legend. There is a 'Christ of the Trades' painting, which depicts Christ surrounded by workmen's tools, including (most appropriately for a clothmaking county) fulling stocks and shears; it has been suggested that the enigmatic message of this painting may be the 'consecration' of honest labour – a theme which will return in the next chapter, when we encounter the saintly George Herbert. Other paintings include the scene at Gesthsemane where the risen Christ is recognized by Mary, and says, 'Touch me not'; a group of angels playing musical instruments; Mary and St Michael weighing a soul in a balance; the death of Mary; and other less decipherable images.

Sculpture, too, played its part in proclaiming the Christian message. There are two outstanding cycles of Biblical sculpture in Wiltshire. Weathering makes it hard now to decipher the scheme of Malmesbury's Norman south porch, but in fact it tells the life of Christ, from

The chancel arch of St Thomas's Church, Salisbury, is filled with the dramatic events of the day of judgement, or doom. It was whitewashed over at the Reformation and rediscovered in the nineteenth century.

A segment of the badly weathered sculpture around the entrance to Malmesbury Abbey porch. The outer orders depict the life of Christ, and corresponding Old Testament scenes fill the inner orders.

annunciation and nativity to ascension and pentecost, in the outer series of vignettes, contrasted with Old Testament anti-types depicted on the corresponding inner orders of the arch. Inside the porch, on either side above the arcading, are the twelve apostles beneath angels, and these have survived in beautiful detail. About a century later the masons of Salisbury Cathedral set about portraying Old Testament scenes for the benefit of the canons who would meet in their chapter house. They are the products of a vivid imagination, and tell us as much about thirteenth-century life and work as they do about the Bible story. But it is probably not these *tours de force* which the Wiltshire church visitor will find the most moving. For me that accolade – and one can only express a personal opinion on such matters – must be reserved for the Saxon virgin and child

Opposite: Details from the cycle of Old Testament scenes portrayed in the frieze above the stalls in Salisbury Cathedral chapter house. Note the vitality of the figures and the enigmatic expression of the three-faced head. *(Reproduced with kind permission of the Dean and Chapter of Salisbury Cathedral)*

The hand of God points down at the Virgin and Child in this powerful eleventh-century sculpture in Inglesham church.

at Inglesham, the delightful church beside the Thames in northernmost north Wiltshire. Mary and her no-longer infant Jesus crouch huddled together in awe, and the hand of God points down at the child's haloed head.

A recurring theme in medieval iconography is the cult of saints. We have seen how the early church resisted but could not overcome the tendency to syncretism, or the incorporation of elements of pagan belief into the Christian scheme of religion. There can be no doubt that many obscure Celtic saints originated as spirit-gods of grove and spring, who were simply christianized. There were links with the classical pantheon, too, such as the identification of St Michael the Archangel with Mercury, the winged messenger of Roman mythology. As a godling of the air and the winds he tends to be the dedicatee of

Aldbourne, a fine example of a medieval church dedicated to St Michael and occupying an elevated site overlooking its village.

churches in high places. Some of his Wiltshire dedications are indeed on elevated sites –
Aldbourne, Brinkworth, Highworth and Tidcombe, for example – but by no means always;
Melksham, Wilsford-cum-Lake, and Little Bedwyn are all close to rivers.

There can be little doubt, however, that church dedications in Wiltshire have something to
tell us about Christian origins. But, unlike counties such as Kent and Leicestershire, no
chronology or explanation has yet been attempted. In Kent it has been noted that by far the
largest group of early dedications is to St Mary, and it is notable in Wiltshire too that many of
the probable early minster churches bear this dedication. Alderbury, Great Bedwyn, Bishop's
Cannings, Calne, Cricklade, East Knoyle, Market Lavington, Marlborough, Potterne, Upavon
and Wilton all have churches dedicated to St Mary. Sometimes a link is fairly obvious, for
example the three Wiltshire churches dedicated to St Swithun (Compton Bassett, Little Hinton
and Patney) were all associated with Winchester; and both the newly founded churches in
Salisbury were dedicated to popular contemporary saints, St Thomas Becket and St Edmund of
Abingdon, the latter a former treasurer of Salisbury Cathedral.

Two other factors relevant to church dedications should be mentioned. One is the tradition
of holding a fair or village revel, or the church-ale described above, on the feast day of the patron
saint. This often led to a saint being favoured whose day was at a congenial or convenient time of
year, and sometimes dedications were changed with a view to switching the date of the feast.

The other factor concerns the cult of saints. We have observed that the canons of
Salisbury Cathedral were eventually successful in having their beloved Bishop Osmund canonised,
with the result that the shrine containing his relics became even more popular as a place of
pilgrimage. Relics were prized possessions in parish churches too. When, at the beginning of the
fifteenth century, the Dean of Salisbury compiled inventories of the possessions of churches in
his care, against Heytesbury he was able to include the following: two crosses containing wood
from the True Cross; ten unknown saints' bones in a small ivory box; St Mary Magdalene's
alabaster box; and a comb and an ivory knife said to have belonged to St Edmund. Calne also
had a comb belonging to St Edmund, and some hair, but this had belonged to St Mary. And at

St Osmund's tomb in Salisbury Cathedral, with knee-holes where pilgrims could kneel in supplication and thanksgiving to the saint.

Durnford there was a little brooch with bones of St Andrew (to whom the church is dedicated) and St Blaise.

Such treasures were kept in a casket or box known as a reliquary, and it has been suggested that the little Norman sculpture reset above the door of Landford church, depicting two figures holding a cross, may have been part of a reliquary which contained a piece of the True Cross, and which was once set above the altar. At Amesbury the abbey church is dedicated to St Mary and St Melor. This reflects the legend that foreign preachers brought from Brittany the relics of an obscure martyred boy-saint, and placed them on the altar in Amesbury church. Miraculously they stuck fast and could not be moved, so the abbess purchased them, and the shrine of St Melor became a place of pilgrimage.

Offerings made at shrines and reliquaries were a useful source of income for cathedrals and abbeys, and their popularity was enhanced by stories of miracles which their respective saints had performed. In Salisbury not only St Osmund, but also the Virgin Mary ('Our Lady of Salisbury'), to whom the cathedral is dedicated, was credited with miraculous powers. In 1421, for example, when the daughter of an affluent citizen fell on to a hot iron spit, and was impaled through the abdomen, prayers to the Virgin and Osmund led to her miraculous recovery, and the thankful family and neighbours went to the cathedral on pilgrimage to give thanks. Miracles at the tomb of St Edith in Wilton Abbey (who had herself brought to Wilton a relic of part of the tip of one of the nails from the cross) were similarly beneficial to the local community, and badges were made for pilgrims venerating the shrines at both Wilton and Salisbury.

The word 'magic' may be springing to mind, and indeed there is a fine line, and one which most medieval worshippers were clearly unable to draw, between prayer (a request for the saint or the deity to effect some desired objective), and magical charm (an automatic effect achieved by association with some ritual activity or artefact). As one enters Oaksey church, near Malmesbury, the eye is immediately confronted by a striking painting of St Christopher carrying the infant Christ across a river. It is on the south wall, opposite the main door into the church. Many, if not most, churches once had such a painting, and it was normally positioned opposite the door, where it could not be missed. In south-east Wiltshire alone St Christopher paintings are known to have existed at Allington, Durnford, Durrington, Idmiston, Wilsford, Winterbourne Earls and Woodford. All except Durnford were destroyed in the nineteenth century. The point about St Christopher was that a widespread medieval belief insisted that anyone who looked upon his image would not die a sudden death that day. Such protection, it appears, was not based on prayer, but on some magic power. It was automatic.

Rather similar was the belief that consecrated church bells had the power to ward off thunder and lightning; and hence the practice of ringing them during a storm. John Aubrey tells

At Oaksey the principal entrance is on the north side, so this gigantic figure of St Christopher was painted on the south wall opposite, where it would be seen immediately by anyone entering the church.

us that the great St Aldhelm's bell in Malmesbury Abbey was rung as a talisman on such occasions. An inscription, he notes, in the nature of a charm, was inscribed on the rim when church bells were cast, and he quotes the Latin version of one. It is almost identical to the inscription on the surviving sixth bell at Broad Chalke, one of the oldest in the county, which is believed to date from the fourteenth century: 'Let wickedness flee when Andrew's bell is striking'. Aubrey knew well the Broad Chalke bells, 'one of the tunablest ring of bells in Wiltshire'.

The cult of saints did not end at the reformation. Ordinary people continued to regard them as local demigods, and pray to them. Aubrey described the dedication of stags horns of unusual size to St Luke, the patron saint of horned beasts, in the chapel of Stoke Farthing near Broad Chalke. He had also been told about old Symon Brunsdon, parish clerk of Winterbourne Bassett (on the Marlborough Downs), who lived until shortly after 1600. The church at Winterbourne Bassett is dedicated to St Katherine, and, 'when the gad-flye had happened to sting his oxen, or cowes, and made them run-away in that champagne- [open-] countrey, he would run after them, crying out, "Good St Katherine of Winterbourne stay my oxen: Good St Katherine of Winterborne, stay my oxen, etc." This old Brunsdon was wont in the summer-time to leave his oxen in the field, and goe to the church to pray to Saint Katherine: by that time he came to his oxen perhaps the gadfly might drive them away: upon such an occasion he would cry out to St Katherine,

Above: Keevil boasts a twelfth-century sanctus bell machined from solid metal. The efficacy of church bell-ringing as a charm against thunder and lightning was widely believed.

Opposite, above: A late-medieval *anthropophagus*, or man-eating monster, at Seend.

Opposite, below: The crude, stylized green man on a Norman capital in St John's Church, Devizes.

as is already here sayd.' And more than 150 years later, in the neighbouring village of Broad Hinton, an unorthodox view of religion was still current. In 1756 some of the church plate was stolen, and the churchwardens let it be known that if the missing property was not returned they would seek the advice of a 'cunning man' from Corsham to trace the culprit. The plate was returned.

All of this brings us to our final consideration, the appearance of secular and even blatantly pagan imagery in Wiltshire churches. We have already stressed the importance of the visual image in a largely pre-literate society, and we can sense the sheer delight of the medieval mason at being allowed to decorate space with grotesque and fantastic figures. There are *anthropophagi* (man-eating monsters) at Seend and Amesbury, grinning monsters at Steeple Ashton, a man with his head in a noose at Berwick St James, an acrobat at Lacock Abbey, even a man apparently smoking a pipe (centuries before they were invented) in Lacock parish church.

Certain popular subjects have no obvious religious connotation, such as the cycle of the labours of the twelve months which is painted on the vault above the high altar of Salisbury Cathedral (see pages vi-ix), or the exuberant and botanically accurate representations of foliage in stone which became popular during the later middle ages. But very often, when we look carefully, a face peers out from between the leaves, and the green man of pagan fertility confronts us. There he is at St John's, Devizes, or again at Durnford, even hiding in

the cloisters at Lacock Abbey (hardly a fit subject for a
nunnery). But the best green man in Wiltshire, who dates from
about 1300, is on a capital at Sutton Benger, near Chippenham.
A doleful but intense figure – with a headache perhaps – he is
mantled with hawthorn, which grows from each side of his
mouth, and birds peck at the berries.

Oaksey's grotesque *sheela-na-gig*.

If the green man represents the fecundity of the plant world, blatant human sexuality is represented by the explicitly female figure known by its Irish name as a *sheela-na-gig*. Until a second one was identified at Stanton St Quintin, and very recently a third at Devizes St John's, the only known Wiltshire example was at Oaksey, high on the exterior north wall close to the church door. It seems hard to credit that this repulsive creature, with gaping sexual organ, could be tolerated for centuries in such a publicly religious place.

But such a paradox is by no means uncommon. And it brings us close to the heart of popular medieval belief. Christianity did not have a monopoly of religion. Indeed the simplistic message of opposing deities, good against evil, Christ versus the Devil, invested in the evil spirits and pagan symbols a form of divinity. And anything with supernatural power had to be respected, even revered. This, to the ordinary man or woman, was not a denial of their Christian faith; it was merely a sensible precaution, an acknowledgement of the spirit world which their parish church had taught was all around them. 'I read somewhere of a shepherd,' recalled Dylan Thomas, 'who, when asked why he made, from within fairy rings, ritual observances to the moon to protect his flocks, replied: "I'd be a damn fool if I didn't!"'

Opposite: The magnificent green man at Sutton Benger. His foliage is so thick and luxuriant that birds have come to feast off the berries.

Establishment Figures

O N 7TH MAY 1553 the churchwardens of St
Edmund's, Salisbury, paid John Atkins sixpence for
pulling down the altar in the vestry and cleaning up
afterwards. It was perhaps an afterthought. The other altars
had been removed several years earlier and replaced by a
communion table. The urgency now was that three days later,
on 10th May, Bishop Capon was due to visit the church, and
it would not do for him to find this relic of popery still in
place. What neither the churchwardens nor the bishop knew
then was that on 21st July in the same year the accounts
would include a payment to the bellringers for ringing, when
'our Soverenge lady mary quene was proclaymed'. And over
the following months further entries would be made,
recording considerable sums spent on mass books, crosses,
new altars and the Easter sepulchre.

Opposite: Monument to Sir Gabriel
Pile and his wife, 1626, in
Collingbourne Kingston church.

It must have been the same everywhere. At Mere the churchwardens' accounts begin in 1556, and in that year over a pound was spent on re-erecting a cross in the churchyard. During the following year the rood loft was mended, and an image of St Michael was paid for. But clearly not everyone was happy about the Catholic backlash of Mary's reign. A note in the accounts records that no new churchwardens were chosen at Easter, 1558, 'by occacon of some varyannce and Contencon amonge certeyn of the parysheners'. The matter was deferred,

The brick church at Farley, completed 1689-90, is one of only a handful of new Anglican churches built in Wiltshire between the Reformation and the nineteenth century.

and became further complicated by Mary's death in November of the same year, 'and by occacon of the Alteracon of some parte of Relygyon, and of the su'yce [service] and Ceremonies of the Churche whiche then ensewyd'. When in 1559 churchwardens were appointed, they had a heavy load of expenditure, which included buying an English Bible, a communion book, psalters, singing books, and the paraphrases of Erasmus; also there was the taking down of the altars and the rood, and 'the defacynge of the Images of the xii Apostles whiche were paynted in the fface of the Rode lofte'. A year later, on the bishop's orders, the rood loft itself was taken down.

The removal and destruction of the apparatus of medieval Catholicism was one of the most significant effects of the reformation for the appearance of our parish churches. Together with the Puritan-inspired vandalism of the following century it has robbed us of most medieval paintings and glass, and much sculpture and woodwork. But the reformation also swept away many of the social institutions which were associated with the medieval church. In particular the abolition of chantries in 1548 severed the link between guilds and fraternities and their parish church, and the disappearance of chantry priests and friaries removed much of the educational and welfare function of religion. Most important of all, the dissolution of the monasteries and redistribution of their property passed control of huge numbers of churches into the hands of laymen — the courtiers, noblemen and *nouveaux riches* of Tudor England.

These 'lay rectors' or 'lay impropriators', as they were known, took the tithes of the parish, but often returned only a fraction for the purposes of religion, in the form of meagre stipends to vicars and curates. What they did contribute, in abundant measure, to their parish churches was not new buildings to the glory of God, but elaborate monuments to the glory of themselves. The number of entirely new churches built in Wiltshire between 1550 and 1800 is very small — Easton Royal in 1591, Sherrington, Standlynch and Farley in the seventeenth century, Hardenhuish (designed by John Wood of Bath) in 1779 — although several others were substantially rebuilt after fire or partial collapse (Marlborough, St Mary, for example, and Sherston's tower).

Hardenhuish church, which stands on rising ground in the parkland of Hardenhuish House, west of Chippenham, dates from 1779 and was designed by John Wood of Bath.

And many of the undervalued clergy, striving to improve their position in a rigidly stratified society, resorted to pluralism ('moonlighting', in current slang) in order to enhance their income. They held several livings, and some of them attempted, either in person or by proxy, to serve them all more or less adequately. The resulting neglect, especially during the eighteenth century, earned the Church of England a bad reputation. As late as the Victorian period anecdotes circulated about the clergy's misguided priorities. At Chilmark, for instance, it was recalled that the rector once asked the clerk to announce: 'Give out that I am unable to officiate next Sunday.' The clerk gave out the notice thus: 'The maister be gwaine a fishing next Sunday, so there'll be no service.' As we shall see in the next chapter, such attitudes provided many an opportunity for dissent to flourish.

The alterations of the 1540s and 1550s, therefore, grudgingly or sanguinely accepted by most parishioners and clergy, set off a chain of events which can be traced through the subsequent three centuries of Wiltshire's religious life, and which will take us right up to the era of the Victorian restorers. At the risk of over-simplifying a vast subject, we may conclude that it was a period when the initiative for evangelism, church-building, and religious experiment passed largely away from the established church, and into the hands of those who chose to worship elsewhere. Its principal legacies to the parish churches which we see today are the elaborate monuments, the gravestones in the churchyard, and, where they have escaped the Victorian restorers, the wooden furnishings – galleries, box pews and three-decker pulpits. We shall also find occasional reminders of the various local government functions which from Tudor times the parish church and parish vestry were called upon to fulfil.

The ninety years or so which separated the 'cleansing of the temple' in the 1550s and the civil war in the 1640s saw, in Wiltshire as elsewhere, a gradual polarization between those whose protestantism was content to rest within the inherited framework of bishops, church authority, clerical robes and a degree of ritual; and those (dubbed Puritans) who felt that the reformation had not gone far enough, and who wished to abolish episcopal rule in favour of government by elders (or 'presbyters'), and to eschew all remaining traces of imagery and popish ritual. Theologically, too, there was a gulf, the Puritans tending towards the Calvinist view, in which the salvation of the elect was predestined; many of the traditionalists preferring an Arminian outlook, which set greater store by good works in the soul's final judgement. The stages by which Puritanism and Presbyterianism evolved as a dissenting movement outside the Church of England will be one of the subjects of chapter six.

For both camps, but especially for the Puritans, religious services were centred on preaching, and so it is to this Elizabethan and Jacobean period that we owe many fine examples of wooden pulpits and lecterns. At Wylye, for example, there is an excellent pulpit dated 1628, which includes a reading desk and a clerk's desk, and an elaborate tester or sounding-board above; it came originally from the now ruined church of St Mary, Wilton. At Odstock, near Salisbury, there are two fine seventeenth-century chairs, as well as a pulpit dated 1580 with the royal monogram, ER, and the motto, 'God bless and save our royal Queen, the lyke on earth was never seen'. We are fortunate, too, in knowing something of the attractive personalities of a few of the country parsons for whom, to use the expression of one of them, 'the Pulpit is his joy and his throne'.

A moving memorial erected by Thomas Crockford, rector of Fisherton Delamere, to a son and daughter who died in infancy.

George Ferebe, for example, was the vicar of Bishop's Cannings between 1593 and 1623. He was an excellent musician, according to John Aubrey, and he was responsible for erecting an organ and teaching some of his parishioners vocal and instrumental music. But not only that: he wrote rustic plays, which were performed by the village to passing royalty; and he organized football matches. Aubrey reckoned that, under his direction, Bishop's Cannings could have challenged all England at music, football and ringing. Thomas Crockford, vicar of Fisherton Delamere near Wylye, had a library of 338 books when he died. In his burial registers (he served Wylye and Stockton as well as his own parish) he added thumbnail biographies in Latin against each name, revealing not only a deep appreciation of human nature, but also an encyclopaedic knowledge of his flock. The personal tragedies which he and his wife Joanna suffered when their first son and third daughter died in childhood are commemorated by a touching little memorial in Fisherton Delamere church.

Ferebe and Crockford, largely unknown outside the county, may be typical of hundreds of others, now completely forgotten. But one Wiltshire clergyman of this period will be remembered as long as hymns are sung and poems are read. This is George Herbert, who, through the influence of his relative the Earl of Pembroke, was presented to the rectory of Bemerton and Fugglestone, between Wilton and Salisbury, in 1630. He only had three years to live, and died aged forty in the rectory house which he restored, opposite the old church at Bemerton. But during his sojourn there he appears to have put into practice the life of a saintly parish priest which he idealized

George Herbert's church, at Bemerton on the western outskirts of Salisbury. Opposite is the rectory which he restored and in which he died.

in his poems, and in his prose work, *A Priest to the Temple, or the Country Parson, his character, and rule of holy life*. Here the weekly round of parish duties is described, and in every sentence Herbert's delight at serving God and his parishioners shines through. In his best known poem, *The Elixir*, which is sung as the hymn, 'Teach me, my God and King', he echoes a medieval idea, the sanctity of work, depicted at Purton as the 'Christ of the Trades' wall painting: 'A servant with this clause, Makes drudgery divine; Who sweeps a room, as for thy laws, Makes that and th'action fine.' And in his instructions to priests he goes so far as to suggest that the country parson should be a lover of old customs, provided that they are good and harmless. If they are not, he should 'pare the apple', leaving his flock the parts that are wholesome.

The attitudes shown by these men, towards, music, drama, literature, sport and folk customs, would all have been anathema to their Puritan brethren. But they do depict the store of humanity and learning to be found in Wiltshire parsonages at this period (and which bred one of the county's most famous sons, Sir Christopher Wren, of East Knoyle); and they come as a welcome antidote to the sorry procession of clerical shortcomings which usually fill the pages of the historical sources.

Nor was religious sincerity restricted to members of the clergy. A study of parishioners' attitude to Anglican worship in seventeenth- and eighteenth-century Wiltshire has concluded that in general they were loyal to the doctrines and liturgy in which they had been brought up, that they took very seriously the Prayer Book's strictures about celebrating communion, and that they were quick to object to a clergyman whom they felt was trying to lead them astray. A tangible reminder of congregational piety is perhaps the curious penitential seat in Bishop's Cannings church. On its wooden back is painted an enormous outstretched hand, which at first glance might appear to be a palmist's *aide-memoire*. In fact the slogans inscribed along each finger and elsewhere are admonitions in Latin, reminding the penitent, for instance, that the hour of his death is uncertain, that he has offended God, and that his plight is wretched.

Thomas Smith, of Shaw near Melksham, was perhaps a typical churchgoer of the gentry class. His diary, kept between 1715 and his death in 1723, shows that he only missed Sunday observance eight times in as many years; that he nearly always noted the text of the sermon in his

The strange penitential seat at Bishop's Cannings. Dire warnings and salutary mottoes in Latin are inscribed on the fingers to admonish the penitent.

diary; and that he peppered its pages with comments of conventional piety. The diary's editor remarks that: 'Thomas Smith can, in fact, be taken as a good representative of anglican morality in the eighteenth century, with its limited social objectives and its emphasis on the stability of society, but its genuine striving after personal honesty and moderation.'

So far we have tried to emphasize some of the positive aspects of parish church life since the reformation. And the 'emphasis on stability of society' also had its positive side. Smith, we discover from his diary, frequently attended the Melksham parish vestry meetings, and involved himself in debates over poor rates and highway rates. This association of the parish church with local government had its roots in the reformation, and the disappearance of medieval institutions which it had brought about. Elizabethan legislation placed various administrative burdens on the incumbent, and on the parish meeting, or 'vestry', and its annually appointed officers, the churchwardens and overseers. These responsibilities included the registration of baptisms, marriages and burials, the care of the parish poor, the relief of vagrants, the control of vermin, the administration of parish charities, various matters concerned with law and order, and the maintenance of roads within the parish. Meetings to discuss these and other matters relating to the church and parish life, to appoint officials and to audit accounts, were held in the church vestry (hence the name) or in the church itself.

Visiting churches today, we sometimes glimpse evidence of their former importance as places of administration. The parish chest, in which documents, registers and other valuables were kept, is often found. Occasionally, as at Britford near Salisbury, the chest is medieval; others are Elizabethan or Jacobean, for example at Great Wishford near Wilton; while very many more in south Wiltshire churches are replacements dating from 1813, and were made at a foundry in Bramshaw in the New Forest. Very common, too, are painted wooden boards hung up in the church, which describe the terms of the various charities for which the churchwardens were responsible. An unusual variant on this theme are the 'bread stones' set into Great Wishford churchyard wall, which proclaim the price of bread at various dates for the purpose of calculating poor relief. Also at Wishford is an example of useful communal property

Parish chests: *(top left)* Britford, late-medieval; *(top right)* Great Wishford, Jacobean; *(above)* Bulford, nineteenth-century, from Bramshaw foundry.

The Great Wishford bread stones.

being stored in the church – a fire engine dated 1728. At Aldbourne there are two fire engines in the church, nicknamed Adam and Eve.

But the 'stability of society' also had a less attractive face. On the one hand the Calvinist theology of predestination, adopted by the Puritans and many dissenting groups alienated from the Church of England, was no respecter of persons. The population was indeed divided into the sheep and the goats, but they could not be identified by worldly dignity such as social class. However, for those left in the established church after the seventeenth-century upheavals, to whom 'good works' was important, personal attainment was seen as a virtue. And as the class structure of towns and villages took on increasing significance, so the parish church, with its ranking of the congregation pew by pew, and its weekly display of 'Sunday-best', became both the mirror and the reinforcement of local snobbery.

The tendency to install fixed pews in churches and then to charge pew-rents had begun in the late middle ages, as we have seen, and after the reformation, when income from the lucrative church ales dried up, these pew-rents became a more important source of church income. In practice, if not always in law, some pews came to be regarded as freehold property, and might be rebuilt to suit the taste and requirements of their owners. The resulting ill-fitting assortment of box pews crammed higgledy-piggledy into many churches offended Victorian sensibilities, as well as being uncomfortable, inconvenient and wasteful of space. They were thus vulnerable to the restorers' hand, and most have gone. But some remain, and the most spectacular collection in Wiltshire is at Old Dilton, near Westbury. Inglesham, in the extreme north of the county, was saved by William Morris from unsympathetic restoration, and it too has retained its pews, as well as an Elizabethan pulpit.

The most notorious and acrimonious dispute over pew ownership in Wiltshire occurred in the minster church at Warminster during the late nineteenth century. Here pews had been held for many years on a variety of tenures, including leasehold, a form of copyhold, and freehold. One of the freehold pews belonged to a prominent dissenting family in the town, the Hallidays, and they objected to its removal when the church was restored in 1887-9. The House of Lords eventually

The parish church could be used to store parish property of all kinds. This fire engine, dated 1728, is inside Great Wishford church.

ruled that it should be replaced, and in 1897 it was fitted up again, only to be removed and smashed to pieces, and a replacement installed under police escort, which survived until 1913.

By their places in church the members of post-reformation parish society were graded throughout their lives, and when they died their status was commemorated by their monument. Effigies and memorial inscriptions were found in medieval churches, too, but then the main purpose, as we have

Few of the high, ungainly and uncomfortable box pews which evolved in churches from the late Middle Ages survived the nineteenth century. Old Dilton, a chapel-of-ease to Westbury, was an exception. Not only do the pews survive, but also two galleries.

seen, was to elicit prayers for the departed's soul. At the
reformation the theology of monuments changed, so that they
became a commemoration of, or tribute to, the life of an
individual. It has been suggested that this shift may be linked
also to renaissance ideas about the importance of the individual,
and it is certainly true that gravestones in churchyards did not

Left: Lydiard Tregoze, Nicholas St
John and his wife, 1592.

Above: West Dean, Borbach
Chantry, the Evelyn monument,
1627.

Above: Aldbourne, Goddard monument, c. 1615.

Right: Salisbury Cathedral, Sir Thomas Gorges and his wife, 1635.

become widespread until the seventeenth century. Ordinary people had previously been buried in unmarked graves, and after their bodies had decomposed no respect was shown to their anonymous bones . But for those who could afford it, and especially for those lay rectors and their families who controlled so many churches, a kind of immortality could be obtained by

WILLIĀ BVTTON ESQ. DYING A. DŃI. MDLXXXX. Æ.T. LXIIII
LEFT BY HIS WIFE MARY DAVGH TO S. WIL. KELLWEY KN.
VI. SONS. AMBROSE KN. WILLIA, WHO MARRIED IANE DA.
TO IOHN LAMBE OF COVLSTO: IOHN, FRANCIS. EDWARD,
& HENRY. II. DAVGHTERS. DOROTHIE MARRIED TO IOHN
DRAKE OF MOVT. DRAKE IN THE COVT. OF DEVO ESQ.
& CECILIE MAR. TO S: IO. MEWYS OF KINGSTO IN THE
ISLE OF WIGHT KNIGHT.
Erected by Sir William Button knight Grand child
to the first William, and Sonne and heire to
the latter, in pious memory.

William Button junior was in no doubt where his grandfather, who died in 1590, would be going when the last trump sounds. This intricate brass memorial is in Alton Priors church near Pewsey.

commissioning fashionable sculptors to erect elaborate memorials inside the church. Taken to extremes a powerful family could almost monopolize a church with its memorials, thus turning it into a kind of mausoleum. In Wiltshire this occurred at Lydiard Tregoze, near Swindon, where the St John family not only took over the church, but also moved the village away to a new site so as to create Lydiard Park.

The earliest of the sumptuous post-reformation monuments follow in the chantry tradition of a recumbent effigy. Such is the Brydges monument at Ludgershall. Later Tudor works might continue this motif, or portray kneeling figures, either facing each other in prayer, or staring out from their memorial. There are good examples at Aldbourne, Collingbourne Kingston, Chippenham, and in the Borbach Chantry at West Dean. The diversity of aspirations may be seen in the two near-contemporary monuments which flank the retrochoir of Salisbury Cathedral. On the south side the Earl of Hertford, who died in 1621, is commemorated by a lofty edifice of overpowering splendour. On the north side the Gorges monument, of 1635, is full of mystical and mathematical symbols, accurately suggesting the eclectic builder of Longford Castle. Later monuments depict figures draped in classical style, with cherubs and angels; of many examples one of the most interesting is the tomb of Thomas Spackman at Clyffe Pypard, which records a native of the parish who made good as a carpenter in London, and endowed a school.

Flamboyant and extravagant memorials may not have impressed everyone. In the churchyard at Froxfield, near Marlborough, there is a simple stone dated 1730, not commemorating anyone in particular, but with a cutting inscription: 'Behold the World is full of Crooked Streets. Death is the Market Place where all Men Meets. If Life was Marchandize that Men could buy. The Rich would always Live the poor must Dye.'

126

Dissenting Voices

Every large organization has its critics, and it is easy to find complaints levelled against the church at most periods of its history. Sometimes the attacks were aimed at individual churchmen, for example the chaplain of Baydon (near Aldbourne) in 1405, who was described as, 'a habitual gossip and causes quarrels between parishioners', one of whom he constantly threatened with a beating. In the same year, it was alleged, his colleague at Winterbourne Dauntsey was 'customarily drunk', and at Chisenbury (near Upavon) the chaplain used to tether his horse to the font. Seven years later the vicar of Burbage, despite living with a woman and keeping a mistress in Salisbury, was accused also of propositioning local servant girls; meanwhile his neighbour at Ramsbury was apparently allowing his vicarage to be used by the rector of Milton Lilbourne for assignations with a woman from

Opposite: The unspoilt interior fittings of Monk's Chapel, near Corsham, built by the Quakers and subsequently taken over as a Congregational chapel.

Marlborough. Parishioners complained if standards dropped too low, but also if they were raised too high. When a Puritan rector arrived at Wylye in 1619 and tried to enforce church attendance, one young lady at first tried sleeping through the service, but then called down a curse on the rector, and went off to a dancing match in the next village.

Such instances could be multiplied *ad nauseam*, but they are only friction generated by the wheels of the great machine. Much more serious were the objections to the church at large, both as an institution and as a theological concept. In the middle ages not everyone was cowed into accepting ecclesiastical authority. The late fifteenth-century doom painting in Salisbury St Thomas, for instance, with its portrayal of a king, a queen and a bishop chained together to be dragged down to hell, can scarcely have enhanced the church's corporate image. It must be seen as a silent protest at what the artist regarded as a corrupt liaison between church and state – the more blatant for it being sanctioned by a congregation worshipping less than a mile from the bishop's palace. And some members of that congregation would have been old enough to remember Bishop Aiscough, and how a Salisbury mob in 1450 had pursued him across the Plain and murdered him at Edington.

The assassination of this hated bishop was part of Jack Cade's rebellion, a protest aimed at both church and state. In its religious aspect it fed on the reforming doctrines of Lollardy, which had been promulgated by John Wycliffe at Oxford in the 1380s, and which became a recurring thorn in the flesh of the later medieval church. There were occasional instances of Lollardy in Wiltshire, including possibly a brief flirtation with its ideals by an Earl of Salisbury, but in general the laity's response to ecclesiastical excesses and neglects was muted. The church was the church. To a remarkable degree this same attitude weathered the turbulent decades of the reformation, and it was only with the growth of Puritanism after 1560 that serious distaste for the established church in Wiltshire began to take hold.

We have already examined Puritan influences on the life of the reformed church. Here we are concerned with the surge of more radical views spawned by Puritanism, which led in time to schism. From about 1600 we begin to hear protests voiced against non-preaching clergy, as at Box on Easter Sunday, 1603, when a weaver and stonemason berated the vicar and denied his ministry. Nearby, at Broughton Gifford and at Slaughterford, groups of disgruntled radicals left their parishes to attend preaching services at other churches, or held religious meetings of their own. At Stratton St Margaret a Puritan churchwarden stirred up resentment in the village by denouncing the non-preaching clergyman to the dean. In Salisbury strong feelings were aroused as religion and local politics polarized around the city's two principal parish churches, the traditional St Thomas's, and the Puritan St Edmund's.

Two influences seem to have fuelled the emerging dissent. At one level the protesters were in touch with radical sects, such as Brownists and Anabaptists, whose members (including Wiltshiremen) were living in exile on the continent. But there was also a social dimension to their protest. John Aubrey's first-hand experience led him to believe that north Wiltshire inhabitants, because they lived on cheese and dairy products, were susceptible to various undesirable traits including, as he noted, 'they are generally more apt to be fanatiques'. And it is quite true that radical Puritanism had an uneven distribution in Wiltshire. It was far more prevalent in the clay or 'cheese' country, and in the towns, especially the cloth-making towns of the north and west. This, we shall see, became a marked feature of later nonconformity.

It was the upheaval of the civil war, and the subsequent years of Commonwealth government, which opened the Pandora's box of religious variety. A purge of traditionalist clergy, and those suspected of royalist sympathies, led to the sequestration of about eighty livings, and the ejection of their incumbents. The majority (predictably) were in the chalkland parishes of south and east Wiltshire, such as Henry Collier of Steeple Langford near Wylye. With his family he was turned out of his house into deep snow. At East Knoyle the rector, Christopher Wren's father (also Christopher), suffered ejection on account of the plasterwork 'pictures' which he had designed for the chancel, and which have survived. The new men who replaced the traditionalists, and those who remained, were Puritans committed to dismantling the hierarchy of the established church, and replacing it with a presbyterian system, based on government by committees of elders. At the same time more extreme dissenting groups, Baptists and Quakers,

East Knoyle's chancel is decorated with plasterwork, which was commissioned by the rector, Sir Christopher Wren's father. As a result of such 'idolatry' he was ejected from his living by the Puritans.

were given a taste of emancipation, and flourished in the sympathetic religious climate.

Putting the lid back on the box, after the restoration of the monarchy and the established church in 1660, was no easy matter. In Wiltshire thirty-one of the more radical clergy were thrown out of their livings immediately, and a further twenty-nine resigned in 1662. They had wrestled with their consciences, and decided that they could not subscribe to everything in the Prayer Book, nor submit to the authority of a bishop, as demanded of them by the Act of Uniformity passed in that year. Here, therefore, were sixty potential threats to the re-established order, influential Presbyterians and Puritans ready, with their supporters, to swell the ranks of other disaffected worshippers, the humble Baptists and defiant Quakers.

At times between 1660 and toleration in 1689 the state hounded dissenters with paranoid ferocity. The persecution, imprisonment and death of Quakers in particular during these years is a sad and shameful chapter in the history of religion. But the degree of persecution varied from region to region, and, apart from the imprisonment of Quakers, Wiltshire nonconformists appear to have endured less than many of their unfortunate brethren elsewhere. This was not as a result of leniency on the part of the Church of England – Bishop Seth Ward (1667-89) was implacably intolerant; it was rather that the dissenting cause embraced a sizeable minority of the population, and included among its friends many sympathetic magistrates. In 1670 Bishop Ward wrote to county magistrates asking them to send him information about unlawful religious meetings (or 'conventicles') held within his jurisdiction. One such letter was received by Sir Edward Bayntun of Bromham, near Devizes, and he, along with six fellow justices, replied to the bishop in bland and unspecific terms, that in their area they could not discover, 'that there hath been any such great and outrageous meetings as were represented'. But of course there had.

In fact, as a result of Bishop Ward's enquiries from clergy and magistrates a document was drawn up listing all the known conventicles, and this cites over sixty clandestine meeting-places active in Wiltshire in 1669-70. Some were shadowy and transient, as suggested by this comment about conventicles at Maiden Bradley, on the Somerset border: 'None of late but there hath formerly been one of Anabaptists. The number about 20. Their quality inconsiderable. Their Teach'r one Robert Cox a Husbandman.' But others were clearly well-established, with large congregations, and a variety of preachers, including ejected clergymen and other educated persons. They met in towns, such as Calne (200-300 Presbyterians), Trowbridge (140-150 Anabaptists), and Bradford (about 200 Presbyterians); but even larger numbers were to be found journeying to lonely places in the countryside, such as Winterbourne Monkton near Avebury, Ferne House near Donhead, Charlcote near Bremhill, and – largest of all – Horningsham, next to Longleat Park, where 600-700 were alleged to hold a 'constant conventicle' in a local clothier's barn.

If in 1669, as was claimed, more than 200 dissenters of various denominations met for worship at St Laurence's Church, Warminster (an Anglican chapel-of-ease overlooking the High

Street), there can have been no secret about it, nor much fear of persecution. But other worshippers had reason to be more cautious, and secluded spots, especially places close to the county boundary, seem to have been favoured. Ditteridge, Grittleton, Colerne, East Knoyle, Homington and Newton Tony were all border parishes with conventicles, as well as Horningsham and Donhead already mentioned. From other sources we hear of similar groups meeting at Stowford and Chilton Foliat. Another border venue was Southwick, between

The implausible datestone on Horningsham chapel reflects a tradition current in 1816 that it was then 250 years old. The building probably dates from about 1700, although there may well have been dissent in the area from a much earlier date.

Trowbridge and Frome, where the local magistrate connived at Baptist meetings, at first on his own land in a wood near Cutteridge, and then in a barn close to the quaintly named hamlet of Scotland. There was, of course, a practical reason for worshipping near boundaries – if the justices approached with a view to breaking up your meeting, you adjourned across the border, beyond their jurisdiction. An extreme example of 'sitting on the fence' has been noted at Downton, where a cottage dating from 1673, probably used for holding conventicles, straddles the former borough boundary; its principal room has a line of stones set in the floor to mark the limit of borough and manor responsibilities.

Immunity from such persecution was not achieved by dissenting protestant groups until the Toleration Act of 1689 (and for catholics not for another century), but hopes of emancipation were growing during the 1670s and 1680s, to such an extent that some Quaker congregations built meeting-houses in anticipation that they would be left in peace. A clue to the extent of pre-toleration building may be derived from the earliest of the certificates which congregations were required to submit under the Toleration Act. During 1689-90 Quakers notified the authorities of meetings in twenty-three separate locations. Twelve were houses belonging to individuals, one was a new-built house within a Quaker burying ground, and ten were described as meeting-houses. These ten lay both in towns (Calne, Devizes, Chippenham and Warminster) and in villages, all in north and west Wiltshire. Presumably, unless any had been fitted up within the space of the previous few months, they had all existed before toleration. Indeed we are told of a meeting house in Chippenham in 1669, and at Cumberwell near Bradford in 1676; tenements on Devizes Green had been bought by Quakers for worship as early as 1647. Two of these pre-toleration meeting-houses still exist. One is an overgrown ruin on a wooded hillside at Slaughterford, near Castle Combe; but the other, at Monk's beside Gastard, near Corsham, is in beautiful condition and still in use, although now by a United Reformed congregation.

The steadfast groups of Baptists, Presbyterians, Congregationalists and Quakers which emerged in 1689 after nearly three decades of proscription are collectively known as the 'Old

Monk's Chapel, near Gastard, Corsham (see also p. 126).

Dissent'. The new freedom which they enjoyed to associate and worship without harassment led to an enthusiastic spate of chapel building, which continued for some fify years until the old dissenting movement had begun to lose its vigour and saw its congregations decline. Traces of this activity survive from all over Wiltshire, although most early chapels have been altered or rebuilt, and some have been demolished in recent years.

The best of the early village or country chapels are at Monk's, which was taken over from the Quakers by Congregationalists, perhaps as early as 1690; at Grittleton, near Chippenham, where the now disused Baptist meeting-house dates from 1720 or slightly earlier; and at Tisbury, where the modest former Presbyterian building dates from 1726. Better known, but extensively altered from their original state, are the Congregational chapel at Avebury of about 1707 (currently the Tourist Information Centre), which stands within the prehistoric henge monument; the Baptist chapel at Bratton, near Westbury, which virtually usurped the Anglican church as the centre of the religious and social life of the village; and the Presbyterian chapel at Horningsham, which probably dates from about 1700. The origins of the congregation meeting at Horningsham, however, are considerably earlier; indeed, when the chapel was extended in 1816 a tradition was fostered that it

Bratton Baptist chapel, near Westbury, built and licensed for worship in 1734, became the centre of the social and religious life of the community, eclipsing the Anglican chapel-of-ease on a hillside outside the village.

was already 250 years old, and a datestone 1566 was accordingly built into the new west wall. No evidence has been found to support this implausible assertion, but on the strength of it the chapel is often claimed to be the oldest in England.

The simple fittings of Horningsham Congregational chapel.

 The architecture of early chapels makes a statement both about the social origins of their builders, and also about their rejection of the ornament and ritual entwined in medieval churches. Village chapels were simple and humble, the embodiment of the honest cottage-dwellers who worshipped in them. In towns too modesty and simplicity might be paramount, as in the little hidden meeting-house off Devizes High Street, built by the Quakers in 1702. But another vernacular tradition, that of the prosperous, no-nonsense clothier, with his foursquare house and (later) his foursquare mill, can also be seen. The old Presbyterian meeting-house of

1704 in North Row, Warminster, later used as a school, looks like a plain but comfortable town house; and the Grove chapel in Middle Rank, Bradford, built by Presbyterians in 1698 and now used by Baptists, is straightforward and severe, made of sturdy ashlar masonry. The first Conigre Chapel at Trowbridge, demolished in about 1857, had a well-proportioned, elegant facade, suiting the wealthy and respectable ranks of nonconformist society which frequented it.

After about 1740 the initiative for chapel building switched from the old dissenting denominations to groups associated with the Methodist revival. As conducted by John Wesley Methodism was not a form of dissent, rather a means of enriching the spiritual life of the established church. But establishment's reluctance to accept the evangelists and their converts led to Methodist societies being formed, and in course of time buildings erected for their meetings. John Wesley's mission began in 1738, and he preached frequently in Wiltshire for more than fifty years, almost until his death in 1791. Early Methodist centres resulting from his work were in the larger towns – Bradford, Trowbridge, Devizes and Salisbury – and in the countryside, notably at Seend, and at Eastcott near Urchfont. Chapels associated with Wesley's preaching survive at Bradford (1756) and Seend (1774), the latter still in use.

One of the most important influences on the young John Wesley was his contact in 1735 on a voyage to America with members of the Moravian church, a movement which had begun as a kind of medieval Methodism in Bohemia during the fifteenth century. They lived communally, and their quiet spirituality and dogged evangelism had a profound effect on the pioneers of the Methodist revival. One of these, John Cennick, who had broken with Wesley on theological matters by 1740, began to preach in north-west Wiltshire with great success, but in 1741 moved on to Swindon, where a mob almost lynched him. Undeterred he established a community along Moravian lines at East Tytherton, near Chippenham, in 1742, and when he left Wiltshire three years later entrusted it to the Moravian church. This little group, of linked chapel, manse, and school, with a separate house for 'single sisters', quietly sits beside an isolated road junction, a short stroll across the meadows from the site of Stanley Abbey, with which it has had a good deal in common.

Of Cennick's other congregations one, at Malmesbury, also adopted Moravian tenets, but most eventually came under the influence of an evangelist named Cornelius Winter. Like Cennick but unlike Wesley, Winter was a Calvinist, and so believed that only the elect were predestined for salvation. The

The modest range of chapel flanked by houses at East Tytherton served the needs of a settlement of Moravian worshippers, established here in 1742.

meetings which resulted from his preaching, and that of his associates, were Congregational (or autonomous) in outlook rather than Methodist, although the term which they generally used to refer to themselves was 'Independent'. And it was they, not the Methodists, who were the most prolific chapel-builders during the half-century after 1750. As evangelists their techniques were similar. They targeted the souls of the farm labourer and the artisan, by holding impromptu services in the open air. As one of Winter's acolytes, William Jay, recalled: '. . . and many a calm and clear evening I have preached down the day, on the corner of a common or upon the green turf before the cottage door'. If the seed of their preaching fell on fertile ground regular meetings were organized in a private dwelling or a barn, and in due course a chapel was built.

The pace of registering new meetings in Wiltshire quickened dramatically as the eighteenth century drew to a close. A tally of nearly four per year in the 1770s rose to six in the 1780s, and an annual average of sixteen during the 1790s. In 1798 alone forty-five buildings were registered for nonconformist worship, at least half of them by Independents. Renewed official hostility to all forms of dissent (fuelled in part by fears of a French-style revolution on this side of the Channel) seemed to give urgency to the cause, especially in Wiltshire. For in 1798 the Bishop of Salisbury declared war on the 'delusions' spread by itinerant preachers, and sparked off a bitter exchange of pamphlets. The nonconformist leaders feared that new restrictions would be placed on their activities, but in the event the controversy died down, and with it the scramble to register new meetings slackened.

Although Independents spearheaded the chapel-building resurgence, their enthusiasm was matched by the emerging Methodist societies, and new life was breathed also into many of the older dissenting congregations. Calvinistic Baptist chapels proliferated, and there was even a modest improvement in flagging Quaker and Presbyterian fortunes. The legacy of this revival may be seen in town and countryside. Independent chapels of the 1790s survive at Corsham (later a printing works), Westbury (Upper Meeting-House) and Wilton, among the towns; and in villages, including Atworth and Winterbourne Dauntsey. There are contemporary Baptist chapels at Bradford (hidden behind a house, and approached through an arch), Westbury Leigh, and

Chapmanslade. And five of the most interesting survivors all date from a few years earlier, 1776-7. The older, hidden portion of the former St Mary's Chapel, Devizes, is exactly contemporary with Providence Chapel at Bradenstoke, next to Lyneham, and with no fewer than three Melksham buildings: the former Quaker meeting-house in King Street (now a Spiritualist church); the Broughton Road Baptist chapel; and the Independent chapel, which has become the Rachel Fowler Centre.

The conflict with the Church of England was defused after 1799, but chapel-building by the various strands of the 'New Dissent' continued. Understandably, many more chapels built during the nineteenth century have survived than from

The Quaker meeting-house in King Street, Melksham, is exactly contemporary with Bradenstoke chapel (opposite). It was subsequently taken over for use as a Spiritualist church.

Providence Chapel at Bradenstoke dates from 1777 and results from the missionary activity of dissenting evangelists, such as Cornelius Winter. Like Bratton, Bradenstoke was poorly served by the Established Church.

earlier periods, and it is possible to see a gradual drift from the straightforward, symmetrical style (often elegant in its simplicity), which was dictated by vernacular tradition, towards the ubiquitous Victorian gothic (or just occasionally classical) designs beloved of the architect's drawing-office, which made their appearance from about 1840.

The rate of chapel formation in Wiltshire between 1800 and 1850 was extraordinary. Nearly twelve hundred premises

Trowbridge, like the other west Wiltshire industrial towns, has many nonconformist chapels. This is Zion Chapel of 1816, one of several ramifications of Baptist dissent in the town.

were registered for dissenting worship during these fifty years, an average of almost one per fortnight. By no means all were used simulataneously, of course; a congregation might register several cottages before building and registering a chapel of its own. Nor were all the result of missionary activity. Nonconformity grew also in the same way as human tissue, by cell division. Doctrinal or procedural disagreements, a controversial choice of minister, personality clashes – for various reasons part of a congregation might secede, and set itself up in its own premises. By 1830 Trowbridge had five substantial Baptist chapels. 'Little Bethel' had broken away from

Penknap Baptist chapel, between Westbury Leigh and Dilton Marsh, one of the 'twenty golden candlesticks' founded from Southwick.

'Zion', which along with 'Bethesda' had broken away from 'Emmanuel', and 'Emmanuel' in turn had broken away from the original Baptist meeting at Conigre, which by then had adopted a Unitarian theology. And denominations themselves might split. Whereas in 1800 a chapel would probably be described simply as Methodist, by 1880 there were Wesleyan Methodists, Primitive Methodists, and Independent Methodists, not to mention the Methodist New Connexion, the Wesleyan Reform Movement, the Bible Christians, and ultimately the Salvation Army, all of them scions of Methodism. Then there were Strict Baptists, Particular Baptists and General Baptists – at Minety the chapel proclaims itself 'Peculiar Baptist'. It is in the nature of dissenters, one must suppose, to dissent.

Architecturally the most interesting achievement of the years after 1800 and before the Gothic revival was that of the Baptists. Southwick was the mother-chapel of a fine group planted along the Wiltshire–Somerset border – 'twenty golden candlesticks', as their historian described them. Penknap Chapel of 1810, at Dilton Marsh, is a good example, and others survive at Trowbridge, Westbury and elsewhere. Strict Baptist preaching in the countryside resulted in a charming group of miniature chapels with Old Testament names. 'Little Zoar' at Derry Hill, near Calne, is picturesque; 'Bethel' at Allington in

'Little Zoar' at Derry Hill, between Calne and Chippenham. It is one of several small Baptist chapels to adopt Old Testament names, and dates from 1814.

Pewsey Vale drew its congregation from a far wider area than its size might suggest, and the 'Cave of Adullam' at Upavon is only matched in obscurity by 'Shecaniah', a Congregational chapel at Christian Malford.

By contrast most of the surviving Methodist and Congregational chapels in Wiltshire result from their proliferation later in the century, and were the work of local architects. Notable among these was W.J. Stent of Warminster. When he died in 1887 a tribute paid to him by the Congregational Union claimed that he had been a prominent figure at all their meetings for more than forty years, and that he had improved or rebuilt, 'nearly all the chapels in the weaker places of our Union, so that in many places our Tabernacles have been exchanged for Temples'. Examples of his work in Wiltshire may be seen at Broad Chalke and Ebbesbourne Wake in the Ebble Valley, at Holt, Westport (Malmesbury) and elsewhere (including the former Sunday School in which this book was written). His most ambitious survivor is perhaps the voluminous chapel at Mere. In this temple worshipped Charles Jupe, local Congregationalism's most influential benefactor.

From the beginning, we have observed, dissent was unevenly spread in Wiltshire. The apparent ubiquity of Victorian chapels tends to mask the fact that nonconformist allegiance and strength continued to vary from region to region. Analysis of meeting-house registrations suggests that, whereas before 1800 missionary activity was still concentrated in the 'cheese' and textile country of north and west Wiltshire (and to a lesser extent around Salisbury), nineteenth-century Wesleyan Methodists began to evangelize the south-east corner, parts of the Marlborough Downs, and Pewsey Vale.

After 1830 Wesleyan vigour waned, and the initiative was taken by the more radical Primitive Methodists. Their campaign, based on centres reminiscent of the Saxon minsters, found receptive souls in areas largely neglected by the Wesleyans. Samuel Heath, who began the Wiltshire mission, made his first base in 1824 at Brinkworth, between Malmesbury and Wootton Bassett. He found Brinkworth, in his words: 'proverbial for its wickedness; deplorable ignorance, glaring vice, and barbarous practices were predominant'. But within little more than a year it was being claimed that missions had been established in eight towns between Chippenham,

Malmesbury, Cricklade and Devizes, and all the villages of note round about. By 1852 some 180 Wiltshire meeting-houses had been registered by Primitive Methodists, spreading from the Brinkworth and Wootton Bassett area to Swindon and the north-east (which was then rapidly filling with engineering workers and their families), down the eastern fringes, and from another centre at Salisbury westward along the Ebble and Nadder Valleys.

The open-air baptistery preserved close to Southwick Baptist church.

In 1851 a religious census was taken, and the report divided most of Wiltshire into eighteen registration districts. There were appreciably more nonconformist chapels than anglican churches in use (395 against 352), and most chapels held an evening service, whereas most churches did not. Taking all services together (and ignoring the likelihood that many worshippers attended more than once) the anglicans mustered a total congregation of nearly 114,000, against the nonconformists' 102,000. But these rather similar totals belie the regional differences. In chalkland districts such as Wilton, Amesbury and Marlborough just over two-thirds (67-70%) of all worshippers attended the Church of England, but moving westward the proportion steadily fell, to under one-third (32%) in the Westbury district, and less than one-quarter (24%) in the Melksham district, which included Trowbridge.

William Doel, pastor of Southwick Baptist chapel, wrote in his history of the chapel that the first anglican building in the village was a small iron church, erected a few years earlier in 1880, and continued:

Thus it will be clearly seen the Baptist Church is the *Established* Church in the village of Southwick, the *State Church* being of very recent date. The Baptist Church existed here at least 225 years before the State Church, and we rejoice to say the Baptist Church is still, as it has always been here, the people's Church, and around its hallowed walls lie awaiting the resurrection morning, the dust of the majority of the inhabitants of this village for near the past 200 years, and we believe this will be the Church of the people for ages yet to come.

Doel published his history in 1890. Thirteen years later a permanent 'state' church was built in Southwick. Conventional in most respects it has one feature possibly unique in an anglican building of the time, an open baptistery for total immersion according to Baptist principles. Such was the nonconformist achievement in Wiltshire.

The juxtaposition of an anglican font and an open baptistery (for total immersion in the Baptist tradition) is the most striking feature of Southwick's anglican church, built in 1903.

The Victorians and After

IT WAS A NOVEMBER AFTERNOON in the year 1887, and at Hilmarton vicarage (which is near Calne) a conversation was taking place between the vicar and one of his neighbours. They were chatting about the current vogue for publishing 'Reminiscences' and memorials of lives. That evening, after his visitor had gone, the Rev Francis Goddard sat down and began to write an account of his own life, which had begun a few miles away in 1814, and was destined to end in 1893, six years after he put pen to paper. His father had been both lord of the manor and vicar of Clyffe Pypard – a 'squarson', as such men had recently been dubbed – and the writer had a vivid recollection of his childhood in that delectable spot beneath the Marlborough Downs. Since that time Clyffe church had been restored and the chancel rebuilt, but the basic structure was unaltered, as it still is today

Opposite: Detail of a buttress on Christ Church, Shaw, near Melksham, a bold essay in the Arts and Crafts style by C E Ponting, 1905.

(although now the visitor approaches through gates made to commemorate the wife of Nikolaus Pevsner, the doyen of architectural historians. In 1983 he was buried beside her in the churchyard.)

But to return to Goddard's childhood, there was, he tells us:

a large family pew, the most commodious and best furnished pew I ever have seen, carpeted, and with a divan all round with stuffed seats. At the doorway two arms, like the arms of a chair or first-class railway seat, terminated the returns of the sittings on each side. The walls were very high, and as children we stood upon the sittings to look over. It was in winter, in spite of the padding, intensely cold. I can recollect how cold now: no stove was then to be found in country churches in general, and this was no exception. The whole was constructed inside the screen of the north aisle, where is now the organ, and as we looked over the top of it, we could see the effigy of the founder under the canopy, half of whose side had been cut away by the village carpenter in order to put in a deal pew for a mason, named Draper.

There seems to have been no question about what career the young Francis would pursue. 'I was destined from early age for the Church, and having, I presume, heard this, a very serious impression was produced in me as to the responsibilities of Holy Orders, even in my youngest years.' So he climbed the educational ladder – beatings at Marlborough Grammar School, bullying and flogging (and cricket) at Winchester College, and then to Oxford, where he learnt to drink wine, but failed to be impressed by the 'stupid tutors', all of them clergymen, but most of them 'steeped in old port'. At Oxford he attended St Mary's Church and heard John Henry Newman preach many of his famous sermons (which he found unedifying), and he became embroiled in a dispute between his college and his bishop over the professor of divinity's lectures.

After Oxford and ordination he was appointed curate, 'sufficiently unfitted for that high office', to Winterbourne Bassett, near his home, which he served from 1837 until 1842. Here, and elsewhere – much to his later regret – he abolished the old choir and parish orchestra. Fifty years later he remembered it with fondness:

The parish clerk, who assumed the leadership in general, stood forward in front of the gallery, which was at the west end, and proclaimed the title and read the first verse of the new or old version of the metrical Psalms. . . One of the instruments then pitched the key, and the fiddlers touched the strings to tune them to it. Then, on the second announcement of the Psalm, all the instruments opened fire, and the nasal harmony began.

By serving the parish as proxy to an absentee incumbent Goddard was a tool of the pluralism which bedevilled the Church of England, and which was gradually being swept away. 'There had been not long before this time,' he recalled, 'men who were galloping curates. I recollect a Mr John Vilette. . . who had churches to serve and passed the intervening spaces always at full speed.' Goddard too was an able rider. He rode over to Marden, ten miles away in Pewsey Vale, each Sunday to take a service; and he also, during his time at Winterbourne Bassett, rode to hounds. But this practice, he admitted, was on the wane, and not many clergymen still hunted.

After spells as curate in parishes outside Wiltshire, and time spent abroad for the sake of his health, he returned in 1849 to take up the living of Alderton, near Sherston. Here, with an annual salary of £80, he married, and his two sons were born; like him, both were destined for the cloth. At Alderton when he arrived the church had just been rebuilt at the expense of the wealthy landowner, Joseph Neeld. This had been accomplished, 'not exactly in the best order of church architecture, nor apparently after the pattern that the architect found existing'. In fact some medieval features left over after the old church was rebuilt found their way into the fabric of the village school.

The £80 stipend was considered meagre by clerical standards, and rising prices during the 1850s tended to devalue it. Nevertheless, 'we contrived to keep a carriage and horse, three maidservants, and a man for groom and gardener; but it was rather a hard battle'. In 1858 he was presented to a more lucrative cure, the living of Hilmarton, and there he remained until his death more than thirty years later.

Francis Goddard's life spanned a period of upheaval in the established church unequalled since the reformation, and his reminiscences touch on many of the topics with which this chapter must be concerned. The old abuses, the dilapidations, theological controversies, church rebuilding and restoration – all have been mentioned and need to be examined. Other matters, such as the conflict with nonconformity, the appeal of catholicism, the reorganization of parishes, and the clergy's pastoral duties, can also be glimpsed in his pages, and in those of his contemporaries.

In the previous chapter we have traced the progress of nonconformity, and now we must consider it from the church's point of view. In general the antipathy between church and chapel was much stronger than it is now. It can be seen in the diary of another Wiltshire clergyman, the normally affable Francis Kilvert, who equated 'dissenter' with 'barbarian' as terms of abuse. Such feelings were mutually held, as he recorded in his diary in February 1874: 'In the meeting house at Kington St Michael a Ranting [i.e. Primitive Methodist] preacher once stated that "the Methodists bring the lost sheep down off the mountains, the Baptists wash them, and the Church of England shears them."'

Goddard, who as a child had been taken to a chapel to see an ecstatic healing service, viewed dissent in a parish as a sign of the clergyman's failure to communicate with his flock. When he broke up the choir at Winterbourne Bassett he recognized his own failure: 'So we lost them and their music and their old twice-a-day church going ways; and they went off, some with their instruments, some without, to the Dissenting chapel.' At Hilmarton several years before he arrived an evangelical curate was succeeded by a vicar of higher-church persuasion, and this led to a rift in the congregation, with some of the best and most religious parishioners leaving to form a Particular Baptist chapel in the village. 'It does not require a very great divergence from the accustomed doctrine to cause a migration from one form to another.'

But of course the divergence between church and chapel was social and cultural, as much as it was doctrinal. And it was hard for sons of squires and parsons to bridge the gulf between themselves and the majority of their parishioners. We have already noted the predisposition for dissent in those parts of the county where small freeholders and industrial workers lived in areas of scattered settlements. Within parishes too a similar geo-graphical divide, along social lines, was present. Goddard's own parish included two principal villages – Hilmarton itself, where most inhabitants lived as tenants in houses recently built by the squire; and Goatacre, originally a community of squatter cottages built on common land. The church, and most church-goers, were at Hilmarton, the 'closed' village. Goatacre, the 'open' village, had Independent and Methodist chapels in

The former Roman Catholic chapel at Bonham, on the edge of the Stourhead estate, which is now a private house.

Goddard's day, and was also a centre of political radicalism. A similar dichotomy can still be glimpsed in many Wiltshire villages. At Luckington and Broughton Gifford, for example, the churches stand aloof at one end of their respective villages; the chapels are at the other end, fronting the village greens.

Religious rivalries were most intense over the matter of schooling. Nonconformists and Anglicans both recognized the efficacy of Sunday schools and dayschools in recruiting adherents, and voluntarily erected buildings to house them, often close to their respective places of worship. Most Church of England schools were affiliated to a body with a tortuous name abbreviated to the 'National Society'; the nonconformist equivalent was the British and Foreign School Society. In Sutton Veny, near Warminster, for example, a National School was

A condition of Lord Arundell's permission to incorporate a Roman Catholic chapel in his house, New Wardour Castle, was that it should not be obvious from outside. It is concealed behind the Venetian window to the left of this picture.

built close to the church in 1850. By 1856 the Congregationalists had begun their own school, which became a British School, and in 1869 provided it with a building next to the chapel. In 1873 a new National School was built, and in about 1908 the British School closed. At Sherston the datestone on the British School is 1844, that on the National School is 1845. Similar battles for young souls were fought in many villages. But perhaps the most vitriolic occurred in Salisbury between 1888 and 1890. It involved not only the nonconformists, led by a local solicitor, but also the Bishop, the Member of Parliament, and government and opposition ministers. The manner in which it was conducted — and eventually won — by the church party bestows little credit on themselves; the Bishop in particular, John Wordsworth, blatantly used his position and wealth to influence the outcome.

A more potent factor in the development of the Victorian church than local squabbles with nonconformists was the growing appeal, for many Anglican clergymen, of the worship and traditions of Roman Catholicism. Under Elizabeth and her successors Catholic families and their priests lived under fear of prosecution for their faith, and were subject to various financial penalties and other restrictions. Locally the old religion was kept alive by a scattering of households throughout Wiltshire, but it was only in one small area of the county, the south-western corner, that recusants, as Catholics who refused to attend their parish churches were known, formed a significant proportion of the population. The toleration afforded to protestant dissenters in 1689 did not apply to Catholics, who continued to be persecuted and discriminated against until emancipating legislation was passed in 1791 and 1829.

Against this hostile background two families in particular promoted Catholicism in Wiltshire, the Stourtons of Stourton, near Mere, and the Arundells of Wardour, near Tisbury. When in 1714 the then Lord Stourton was forced to sell the ancestral home, which had remained Catholic since the Reformation, the congregation moved to a medieval chapel attached to the nearby manor house at Bonham, in remote wooded country close to Stourhead and the Somerset border. Wardour Castle, the home of the Arundells, was rendered uninhabitable during the civil war, but a chapel was refurbished in the ruins, and sufficed until the family had recovered its

fortunes sufficiently (by a series of judicious marriages) to build the present mansion in 1770-6. At this period the Catholic services held at Wardour were said to attract the largest congregations in England outside London, and so, although emancipation was still twenty years away, New Wardour Castle was designed to incorporate a magnificent Palladian chapel. In fact the Arundells had obtained a special dispensation from George III to build their chapel, on condition that no outward signs of it were visible; this explains also its insignificant entrance. When it was new, in 1780, the chapel was said to serve 540 Catholics, rather more than half the Wiltshire total at that date. From Wardour Jesuit missionaries were sent to Salisbury, and used the house in the Close still known as Arundells, before registering a series of chapels. In 1848 the present St Osmund's Church in Exeter Street, designed by Pugin, was opened.

Augustus Welby Pugin provides the link between Catholicism in Wiltshire, the Tractarian controversy, and the spate of new churches and church restorations which we shall shortly consider. An unstable genius, who died insane, Pugin settled at Alderbury in 1835 after he had been converted to Catholicism, and built himself a large house which still exists, St Marie's Grange. Here he wrote *Contrasts*, an influential book which extolled the virtues of Gothic (that is, pointed medieval) architecture over the styles currently in favour. The book was illustrated with examples of his fine draughtsmanship, depicting buildings in accurate detail. This interest in the minutiae of

Opposite: The sumptuous interior of Wardour's Catholic chapel, completed in 1776.

medieval architecture, and the attempt to understand and classify its progress, had been pioneered a few years earlier by another man associated with Wiltshire, the antiquary John Britton. But Pugin was as concerned with the traditional religion bound up in the architecture as in the architecture itself, and this notion appealed to the leaders of the Tractarian movement, Newman, Keble and Pusey, whose crusade to restore Catholic ideas of ritual and theology was just then gathering momentum. The synthesis of high church ideals and medieval architecture was christened 'ecclesiology', and this involved not only the scholarly analysis of existing medieval churches, but also the erection of new ones, faithful to the principles such analysis had determined.

Whether the average country clergyman was greatly impressed by Tractarianism is another matter. Francis Goddard, who, we recall, had attended Newman's famous sermons, was unmoved: 'I never heard any of the undergraduates who attended St Mary's with myself discuss those sermons. I am inclined to think that, like myself in my ignorance, they did not understand them: all the divinity put into our hand had an opposite tendency.' Goddard's position seems to have been pliant. The Bishop of Salisbury at that period embraced low-church principles, 'and as I was destined to become a clergyman of the diocese of Salisbury, some of the theology that I was required to get up was of that school'. Kilvert, likewise, was not a high-churchman, and he disapproved of theatricality in worship, but Catholicism was not anathema to him. In September 1875 he visited the Catholic church in Bath: 'I knelt in the church and prayed for charity, unity, and brotherly love, and the union of Christendom. Surely a Protestant may pray in a Catholic church and be none the worse.'

Whatever equivocation may have existed within the realms of theology, in architecture the Gothic style (with the occasional experiment in Norman Romanesque) became almost *de rigueur* by the 1840s. And its impact was enormous. Tractarianism, Pugin and ecclesiology coincided with a wave of church building and rebuilding unrivalled since the twelfth century. This was stimulated, in part, by the growth and redistribution of population that was occurring, but it also reflected the church's eventual recognition that many of its buildings were on the point of falling

One of the new churches of the 1830s and 1840s built to cater for the growing suburbs of Wiltshire's industrial towns. This is Holy Trinity, Trowbridge, and dates from 1838.

down. And it was made possible by new arrangements for managing church finances (under the Ecclesiastical Commission, set up in 1836), and for the easy creation (after 1843) of new parishes and church districts out of the medieval dinosaurs. Thus from the 1830s onwards there would be new churches on new sites, new churches replacing old churches, and old churches made good as new.

In Wiltshire the process of building churches in new locations began in 1836, with the erection of the first of the

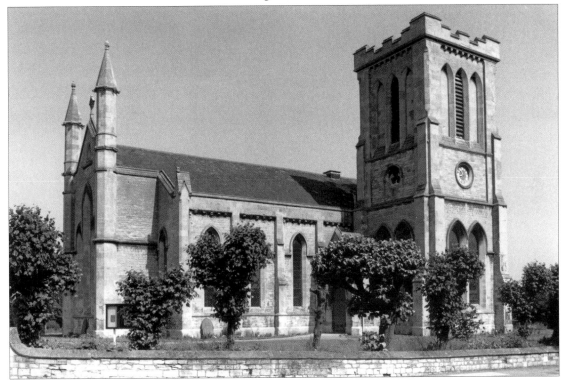

St Mark's, Swindon, 1843-5, was built with the encouragement, although not at the expense, of the Great Western Railway. It served the railway village created alongside the company's engineering works.

'suburban' churches in expanding towns. This was Christ Church, Warminster, and it was followed by Holy Trinity, Trowbridge (1838), Christ Church, Bradford (1841), and St Mark's, Swindon (1843-5), all variations on the Gothic theme. The year 1837 saw the first village church, St Mary's, Redlynch, built to serve a new ecclesiastical district carved from its parent, Downton. After 1843 the splitting of other large parishes, such as Westbury and Great Bedwyn, took place. Out of Westbury three new parishes – Bratton, Heywood and Dilton Marsh – were created, and two were given new churches; Dilton Marsh

Holy Trinity, Dilton Marsh was built in 1844 as a parish church to replace the chapel-of-ease at Old Dilton. Its architect, the prolific T H Wyatt, flirted briefly with this heavy Norman style during the 1840s.

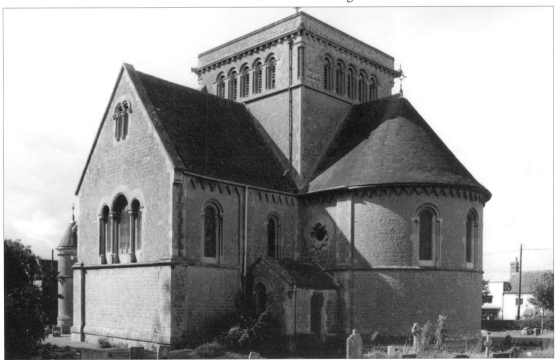

St Nicholas, East Grafton, is
another 1840s Norman style
church, by another prolific Victorian
architect, Benjamin Ferrey.

dates from 1844, and is solid Norman in style, but Heywood, five years later, is Gothic, with an elaborate Decorated east window (which Pevsner, incidentally, described as, 'especially horrible'). Another church in Norman style, and also of 1844, is at Grafton, a parish formed out of Great Bedwyn. Here the principal benefactor, Lord Bruce, was so enthusiastic that he entered the church with a friend to inspect the new roof, before the mortar had dried. It fell on them and killed his friend, a visiting clergyman.

The short-lived vogue during the 1840s for Romanesque architecture, as opposed to Gothic, which these Norman-style churches display, has also left Wiltshire with one of its most remarkable buildings, the parish church of St Mary and St Nicholas at Wilton. Its slender campanile and Italianate basilica, a treasure-house of Roman and medieval antiquities brought

Opposite: Wilton parish church, T. H. Wyatt's extraordinary essay in Italian Romanesque, built for Sidney Herbert between 1841 and 1845, and incorporating works of art brought back from the continent.

back from Europe by Sidney Herbert, could not be more incongruous in the so-called 'ancient capital of Wessex'. It was built between 1841 and 1845 by the architect T.H. Wyatt, who also designed Dilton Marsh, as well as many Gothic churches in the diocese. Unlike Dilton Marsh it was probably not a new church on a new site, since its dedication reflects the belief that

The Tractarian ideal, Mozley's church at Cholderton. Begun in 1841, funding difficulties meant that its opening was delayed until 1850, several years after Mozley had left the parish.

the medieval church of St Nicholas had stood nearby. And its completion meant the end of the old St Mary's long career as Wilton's principal parish church. Most of it was demolished, but the chancel and forlorn skeleton survive in the market place.

Sidney Herbert, who paid for the extravaganza, was of course fully aware of the Tractarian influence on church architecture. Not a Tractarian himself, he was nevertheless a friend from Oxford days of one of the most committed of them, Newman's brother-in-law Thomas Mozley. Mozley was appointed rector of Cholderton, in the Bourne valley, in 1836, and soon had plans to demolish the existing medieval church (which may have had Saxon features), and replace it with a new building in the same churchyard. T.H. Wyatt was chosen architect, and the style was to be Perpendicular, because Mozley had purchased a fifteenth-century hammer-beam roof in Suffolk in 1840, and wished to incorporate it in his new church. The church was begun in 1841, despite opposition from local landowners and the patron of the living, Oriel College. Mozley, forced to pay for it himself, ran out of money and work stopped for a time; but then he began to finance the project by writing as a journalist for the *Times*. In 1847, the church unfinished, he left Cholderton, but continued to pay for its completion, and it was opened in 1850. The planned Tractarian interior was disallowed by the bishop, but the building – looking more like a college chapel than a country parish church – remains as a monument to the tenacity of an ideal.

Twelve new churches were built in Wiltshire between 1836 and 1851, and another twenty by 1862. Thereafter the tally was fourteen more by 1887, and only another eight up to 1953. The money to pay for all this activity, as well as more than 250 rebuildings, restorations and enlargements, came from various sources, including local landowners and patrons, wealthy incumbents, fund-raising by parishioners, and a variety of grant-making bodies, at diocesan and national level. The resulting edifices, therefore, reflect not only the stylistic preferences and competence of the architects responsible, but also the tastes of their paymasters.

Sutton Veny church, near Warminster, was begun in 1866 in memory of a member of a local family of clothiers and landowners, the Everetts. It was paid for by the family, who engaged one of the most competent and respected of London architects of his day, John Loughborough

Pearson. He had a distinctive style, which included stone vaulting and a spire, and the result is a handsome and memorable church. Pearson was also responsible for two churches in east Wiltshire close to the Hampshire border, at Chute and Chute Forest. They are of brick and flint, and both have spires.

St Katharine's, in Savernake Forest, displays the wishes of the client as much as the skill of the architect. Like Wilton it was designed by T.H. Wyatt for a member of the Pembroke family (who had married into the Ailesburys); its aristocratic lines, idiosyncrasies, broad carriage drive to the entrance, and position in a remote corner of a large estate, all point to what it was designed to be – the private church of a powerful clan.

Other churches had different aspirations. St John's, Boreham (1865) was built by Canon Sir James Erasmus Philipps, Tractarian vicar of Warminster (and an adept fundraiser), partly to serve the expanding suburb; but also, it seems, so that he could indulge his taste for very high church services there with fewer inhibitions than at the minster. St Mark's, Swindon, was also high church in its leanings, and under the redoubtable Canon J.M.G. Ponsonby (vicar 1879-1903) its congregation built no fewer than four district churches and one new parish church to serve the burgeoning industrial town. One of these, St Saviour's, was a wooden church constructed in 1889, in just over six months, by railway workers in their spare time. The original building was encased in stone and reopened in 1961.

The task of evangelizing remote hamlets, so successfully undertaken by nonconformist groups (especially the Primitive Methodists) earlier in the century, was now taken up by the established church. Some were designed by well-known architects, and obeyed more or less the canons of the Gothic revival; Cadley in Savernake Forest by T.H. Wyatt, and Oare near Pewsey, by Samuel Teulon, are somewhat wayward examples. Others were more rudimentary, and some could even be mistaken for nonconformist chapels. The most unusual, perhaps, is the thatched wooden church at Sandy Lane, built in 1892, which can be glimpsed behind trees from the Devizes–Chippenham road. A surprising number of these small district churches have survived; and although edifices such as the iron mission church of 1905 at Brokerswood (near North

Sutton Veny church, of 1866-8, was built at the expense of the Everett family. It is an impressive and lavish building, designed by one of the most stylish of the Victorian church architects, John Loughborough Pearson.

This anglican mission church at Brokerswood originally stood at Southwick, where it replaced a building destroyed by fire in 1897. It was moved to its present site in 1904 and, when photographed, looked resplendent in fresh green paint.

Bradley), St Matthew's, Mere Woodlands (1882), St Mary Temple at Whitbourne, near Corsley (1903), and the wooden mission hall at Landford Wood on the edge of the New Forest, can by no stretch of the imagination be described as great architecture, yet they still must take their place in the panoply of the Church of England's crusade into the countryside.

But the erection of new churches, large and small, was only one aspect of the Victorian achievement. Far more numerous, as we have seen, were enlargements, rebuildings and restorations. In fact a church untouched by the hand of the restorer is a rarity. The work ranged from minor refurbishment by a sympathetic antiquarian, to wholesale demolition and rebuilding. Most restorations took place during forty years or so after 1850, but Wiltshire boasts a notable effort, Gothick rather than Gothic, from several decades earlier. This is the exquisite church of St John Baptist, Mildenhall, near Marlborough, which in 1815-16 was provided with sumptuous wooden furnishings, including new pews, panelling, reredos, gallery and pulpit, all at the expense of, and in the taste of the wealthy rector, Charles Francis. Although he died when Francis

The pre-Victorian restoration and fittings of Mildenhall church date from 1815-16, and are in 'Gothick' style. They were undertaken on the initiative of the wealthy rector, Charles Francis.

Goddard was about seven, he thought that he remembered Francis attending the christening of his brother; what stuck in the young Goddard's mind was the quality of this affluent clergyman's trousers, which were made of Nankeen, a fashionable yellow cotton.

Charles Francis was clearly a man of flair, but the Victorian restorations were generally more humdrum. The procedure for restoring a church was usually the same, and can be illustrated by a pair of examples. At Patney, in the heart of Pewsey Vale, the rector in 1875 (presumably following discussions with interested parties) approached a local architect, Henry Weaver of Devizes, to draw up a plan of the existing church, elevations and plans of proposed alterations, and a specification of the proposed works, with costs. These were discussed by the parish vestry in February 1876, and a new specification was drawn up to accompany a 'faculty petition', or request to the diocesan authorities to allow the work to proceed. The petition explained that the church and chancel were in general decay, the nave was disfigured by an unsightly gallery, and the pews afforded insufficient space for kneeling. The roof was in need of repair, and the chancel arch and walls were out of upright. In addition to repairing all these defects, it was proposed to refloor and repew the church, to erect a new screen and other wooden fittings, and to install heating apparatus. Once the faculty had been granted, in July 1876, a contract was drawn up with a firm of builders from Bromham (March 1877) and the work was put in hand. In February 1878 a service was held to mark the reopening of the church, and the local newspaper reported that the architect, 'had paid great attention to the restoration of the style of the original'. The work cost about £1,100, almost twice the original estimate.

Two years later the process began at Hilmarton, and Francis Goddard recalled the circumstances:

Mr Poynder [the landowner] had long talked of doing something considerable to the church, which although in good repair in general had but few features of beauty in it, and the columns of which were, and had been from time immemorial, declining greatly from the perpendicular, as much in fact, as one foot from the capital to the base.

He describes a meeting over luncheon at the vicarage between Mr Poynder, his agent, the eminent London architect Mr George Edmund Street, and himself. After lunch Street surveyed the building, while Poynder and Goddard looked on, suggesting possible improvements.

> Mr Poynder warmed to the subject, and said [to Goddard], 'Now let us hear what you really do want to be done, and we will instruct Mr Street accordingly.' So eventually Mr Street countermanded his carriage for a later train, called up the builder he had brought with him, carefully examined every part of the building, and departed with his plans.

As his memorial implies, the lord of Hilmarton manor did not live to see the result of his munificence.

IN MEMORY OF
WILLIAM HENRY POYNDER
ESQUIRE.
OF HILLMARTON AND HARTHAM PARK
IN THIS COUNTY.
WHO DEPARTED THIS LIFE
ON THE 3RD OF AUGUST 1880.
AGED 59 YEARS.

"HE IS OUR GOD, EVEN THE GOD OF WHOM COMETH SALVATION.— BY WHOM WE ESCAPE DEATH." PSALM LXVIII. 20TH VERSE.

THE RESTORATION OF THIS CHURCH
WAS BEGUN BY HIM IN 1879
AND COMPLETED IN 1881.

And that was the last that Poynder and Goddard heard of the matter for nearly a year, until in desperation Goddard actually took a trip to London to Street's office, and made him find the plans. The building work then began, but Poynder, who was paying for it, died shortly afterwards, while the church was still in ruins, and the funeral service had to be held amid the rubble. Street himself died not long after the restoration was complete.

By 1900 the impetus for restoring churches and building anew had passed, so that by comparison Wiltshire has relatively little church architecture to show for the twentieth century. There is, it is true, a fine essay in turn-of-the-century Arts and Crafts style at Shaw near Melksham. It is a rebuilding in 1905 of a Wyatt church of 1838, and was paid for by the owner of Shaw Hill House. The architect, Charles Edwin Ponting, who lived at Overton and practised at Marlborough, had done more

Opposite: Ponting's bold essay in Edwardian Arts and Crafts style, dating from 1905, is at Shaw, near Melksham (see also page 148).

than anyone in Victorian Wiltshire to understand old churches and to restore them sympathetically; at Christ Church, Shaw, he was able to demonstrate his skill as an imaginative craftsman of the first order. There is another Arts and Crafts Movement church by Ponting at Morgan's Vale, near Downton.

After Shaw, the sturdy but traditional garrison church at Bulford Camp (1920-7) comes as a disappointment. Its counterpart at Larkhill (1937) is unmistakeably in the twentieth-century 'Odeon' tradition, and can be compared with the more stylish St Francis's, in Castle Road, Salisbury. With the

Pevsner described Bulford's garrison church as 'smug'.

St Francis's Church, Salisbury, was built in 1936-9 to serve a growing middle-class suburb north of the city.

post-war churches of housing estate and urban redevelopment, such as St Paul's, Covingham, and St Aldhelm's, in Swindon town centre, we seem to have entered a different world.

Or have we? Let us hope that, if St Aldhelm could make the journey from Malmesbury to Swindon, from the seventh century to the twentieth, and see the unostentatious church that is dedicated to him there, he would approve of the continuity of Christian purpose and human endeavour which it represents. Just as we, who in this book have made that same journey, can appreciate the continuous, if sometimes tangled, thread of Christianity and humanity woven into the churches and chapels which we see around us.

St Aldhelm's, Swindon, was built in 1967-8 close to the principal shopping streets of the modern town, but its dedication takes us back almost to the beginnings of Christianity in Wiltshire.

Three Norman Tympana: at Knook
(*top*); Little Langford (*centre*); and
Whaddon (*bottom*)

176

Epilogue: Visiting and Photographing Churches

IN OUR PREFACE we suggested that this was a book for the ordinary church visitor. And so it is. But that does not mean that the churches are ordinary, nor that visiting them need be an 'ordinary' experience. We hope that, having read the text and studied the illustrations up to this point, you the reader will have reached the same conclusion.

Exploring and understanding the past is generally a matter of asking and trying to answer questions. In this brief epilogue we list some of the questions which the church visitor (or, for that matter, the potential church guidebook writer) might ask of the evidence. The quest to find answers should help to place any particular church into some kind of context, much in the way that this book has attempted for Wiltshire churches in general. Also in this epilogue are brief notes on photographing churches, and on the photographs in this book.

Here, then, are some questions:

TOPOGRAPHICAL

§ How does the position of the church relate to the settlement and parish which it serves?

§ What shape is the churchyard, and does it contain any special features or peculiarities?

§ How do the church and churchyard relate to neighbouring properties, plots of land, and rights of way?

§ Is the church part of a larger complex, including for example school, rectory, manor house, or church house?

ARCHITECTURAL

§ Are there relict features of antecedent buildings, such as a display of Roman or Saxon fragments?

§ What are the main building periods, and how do they relate to the wealth of owners, patrons and parishioners?

§ What medieval and post-reformation fittings have survived Victorian restoration?

DEVOTIONAL

§ Is there evidence of the ritual or liturgical functions of parts of the building, such as the position of altars or windows?

§ Are there chantry or guild chapels, and if so what were the circumstances of their foundation?

§ Are aspects of medieval belief, including latent paganism, preserved in wall-paintings, sculpture or glass?

§ Does the church have an unusual dedication?

SOCIAL

§ What do monuments tell us about the leading families in the parish?

§ Is there any evidence of parish government, such as charity boards, a parish chest or other communal property?

§ If the church underwent Victorian restoration was this for structural reasons, a need for more accommodation, or the theological leanings of a long-serving incumbent?

THE PHOTOGRAPHS

Almost all were taken during 1992/3 with an Olympus OM camera fitted with a 35mm PC (Perspective Control) lens using FP4 plus film. Occasional use was made of 24mm, 135mm and 450mm lenses. Tripod and flash were used where necessary, but all outside views were hand-held.

With nearly two hundred churches to photograph in one year it was not always possible to choose ideal lighting or weather conditions, and so certain pictures have been used to illustrate a particular church or detail which are not quite up to the desired standard.

Although black and white photography is generally easier than colour (slides), church interiors often present problems of extreme contrast. Bright sunshine streaming into a dark church can present insurmountable problems, even when supplementary flash is used to lighten shadow areas. Preferred conditions are when the sun is obscured by light clouds giving so-called 'cloudy-bright' illumination.

Finally, church photographers should remember that churches are usually not heated, so warm clothing is desirable, even at times in summer.

Bibliography

WITH A FEW ADDITIONS published since 1993 this bibliography is that prepared for the first edition of this work. Considerations of space, however, resulted in it being greatly curtailed, and only now is it printed in full. The bibliography begins with a few general works which are relevant to the whole, or large parts, of this book, and without which it could not have been written. The more important sources for each chapter then follow.

General

Bettey, J.H., 1979, *Church and community: the parish church in English life*

Bettey, J.H., 1987, *Church and parish: an introduction for local historians*

Morris, Richard, 1989, *Churches in the landscape*

Pevsner, Nikolaus, 1975, *Wiltshire*, revised ed. by Bridget Cherry (The Buildings of England)

Pounds, N.J.G., 2000, *A history of the English parish*

Pugh, R.B., and Crittall, Elizabeth (eds.), 1956, *A history of Wiltshire*, vol.3 (Victoria History of the Counties of England)

Rodwell, Warwick, 1981, *The archaeology of the English church: the study of historic churches and churchyards*

Royal Commission on Historical Monuments, 1987, *Churches of south-east Wiltshire*

(in addition, volumes of the *Victoria history of Wiltshire*, the *Wiltshire Archaeological and Natural History Magazine* (hereafter abbreviated as *WANHM*), and the Wiltshire Record Society have been used throughout)

Christian Origins

General: Blair, John (ed.), 1988, *Minsters and parish churches: the local church in transition, 950-1200*

Darlington, R. R., 1955, 'Anglo-Saxon Wiltshire', *Victoria History of Wiltshire*, vol.2, 1-34

Haslam, Jeremy, 1984, 'The towns of Wiltshire', in Haslam, Jeremy (ed.), *Anglo-Saxon towns in southern England*

Stone, L., 1955, 'Anglo-Saxon art', *Victoria History of Wiltshire*, vol.2, 35-41

Taylor, H. M., and J., 1965-78, *Anglo-Saxon architecture*, 3 vols.

Thomas, Charles, 1981, *Christianity in Roman Britain to AD 500*

Watts, Dorothy, 1991, *Christians and pagans in Roman Britain*

Alderbury: Chandler, John, 1987, *Salisbury and its neighbours*

Bishopstrow: Powell, J.U. 1903, 'The early history of the upper Wylye Valley', *WANHM*, vol.33, 109-31

Box: Hurst, Henry, et al, 1987, 'Excavations at Box Roman villa, 1967-8', *WANHM*, vol.81, 19-51

Bradford on Avon: Corney, M, 2003, *The Roman villa at Bradford on Avon: the investigations of 2003*

Castle Copse: Hostetter, Eric, 1985, 'Preliminary report on excavations at Castle Copse, Great Bedwyn, 1983-4', *WANHM*, vol.79, 233-5

Hostetter, Eric, and Howe, Thomas N., 1986, 'Preliminary report on excavations of the late Roman villa at Castle Copse, Great Bedwyn, 1985', *WANHM*, vol.80, 97-102

Ward, John, 1860, 'Great Bedwyn', *WANHM*, vol.6, 261-316

Cherhill/Manningford Bruce: Johnson, Peter, and Walters, Bryn, 1988, 'Exploratory excavations of Roman buildings at Cherhill and Manningford Bruce', *WANHM*, vol.82, 77-91

Codford St Peter: Swanton, Michael, 1979, 'The "dancer" on the Codford cross', *Anglo-Saxon Studies in Archaeology and History*, vol.1, 139-48

Cricklade St Mary: Haslam, Jeremy, 1982, 'A "ward" of the burh of Cricklade', *WANHM*, vol.76, 77-81

Latton: Passmore, A.D., 1943, 'Roman stones at Latton', *WANHM*, vol.50, 293

Market Lavington: Anon, 1992, 'Excavation and fieldwork in Wiltshire 1990', *WANHM*, vol.85, 156-62

Marlborough St Mary: Wordsworth, Christopher, 1905, 'A relic of pagan Marlborough', *WANHM*, vol.34, 205-7

Nettleton: Wedlake, W.J., 1982, *The excavation of the shrine of Apollo at Nettleton, Wiltshire, 1956-1971*

Potterne: Davey, Norman, 1964, 'A pre-conquest church and baptistery at Potterne', *WANHM*, vol.59, 116-23

Davey, Norman, 1990, 'Medieval timber buildings in Potterne', *WANHM*, vol.83, 57-69

Purton: pers comm. Chris Chandler and Jill Jefferson Jones

Tidworth: Goddard, E.H., 1921, 'Roman lamp with cross emblem, Tidworth', *WANHM*, vol.41, 424

Wroughton: Thomson, T.R., 1956, 'The bounds of Ellandune, c. AD 956', *WANHM*, vol.56, 265-70

The Parish Church Takes Shape

General: Pevsner, Nikolaus, and Cherry, Bridget, 1975, *Wiltshire*, 2nd ed. (The Buildings of England)

Rodwell, Warwick, 1981, *The archaeology of the English church: the study of historic churches and churchyards*

Royal Commission on Historical Monuments, 1987, *Churches of south-east Wiltshire*

Templeman, G., 1956, 'Ecclesiastical history 1087-1547', *Victoria History of Wiltshire*, vol.3, 1-27

Bishopstone: Salzman, L.F., 1952, *Building in England down to 1540* [p.404]

Compton Bassett: Reynolds, Andrew, 1993, 'A survey of the parish church of St Swithun at Compton Bassett, Wiltshire', *WANHM*, vol.86, 102-12

Dean Chandler: Timmins, T.C.B. (ed.), 1984, *The register*

of John Chandler, Dean of Salisbury, 1404-17 (Wiltshire Record Society, vol.39)

Taxation, 1334: Hoskins, W.G., 1959, 'Economic history', *Victoria history of Wiltshire*, vol.4, 1-6

NOTE: Most examples have been drawn from topographical volumes in the *Victoria history of Wiltshire* series, from RCHM, 1987 (see above), and from miscellaneous notes collected by the author for his history of Wiltshire, of which two volumes have been published so far: *Marlborough and Eastern Wiltshire*, 2001; and *Devizes and Central Wiltshire*, 2003.

The Specialist Church

General: Aston, Mick, 2000, *Monasteries in the landscape*

Edwards, Kathleen, 1956, 'Cathedral of Salisbury', *Victoria History of Wiltshire*, vol.3, 156-210

Midmer, Roy, 1979, *English medieval monasteries (1066-1540): a summary*

Platt, Colin, 1984, *The abbeys and priories of medieval England*

Pugh, Ralph B., and Crittall, Elizabeth (eds.), 1956, *Victoria History of Wiltshire*, vol.3 [includes articles by various authors on religious houses in Wiltshire; see also Edwards, 1956, above]

Amesbury: Royal Commission on Historical Monuments, 1987 [see chapter two]

Bishops' Activities: Horn, Joyce M., 1982, *Register of Robert Hallum, Bishop of Salisbury 1407-17* (Canterbury and York Society, vol.72)

Sandell, R.E., 1976, 'Two medieval bishops and their wanderings', *Hatcher Review*, no.1, 19-25

Wright, D.P., 1985, *Register of Thomas Langton, Bishop of Salisbury 1485-93* (Canterbury and York Society, vol.74)

Bradenstoke: London, Vera C.M. (ed.), 1979, *The cartulary of Bradenstoke Priory* (Wiltshire Record Society, vol.35)

Bradford on Avon: Harvey, R.B. and B.K., 1993, 'Bradford on Avon in the 14th century', *WANHM*, vol.86, 118-129

Dean's Visitation: Timmins, 1984 [see chapter two]

Edington: Stevenson, Janet H., 1987, *The Edington cartulary* (Wiltshire Record Society, vol.42)

Leland: Chandler, John, 1993, *John Leland's itinerary: travels in Tudor England*

Malmesbury: quotation from Pevsner and Cherry, 1975

Old Sarum: Royal Commission on Historical Monuments, 1980, *Ancient and historical monuments in the city of Salisbury*, vol.1

Prebends: Stewart, Pamela, 1973, *Diocese of Salisbury: guide to the records . . .* (Wiltshire County Council, Guide to the Record Offices, pt.4)

Pre-Conquest Dioceses: Darlington, 1955 [see chapter one]

Stenton, F.M., 1971, *Anglo-Saxon England*, 3rd ed.

Ramsbury: Croucher, Barbara, 1986, *The village in the valley: a history of Ramsbury*

Salisbury: Chandler, John, 1983, *Endless Street: a history of Salisbury and its people*

Images of Belief

General: Anderson, M.D., 1955, *The imagery of British churches*

Aubrey, John, 1847, *The natural history of Wiltshire* (edited by John Britton)

Aubrey, John, 1972, *Three prose works* (edited by John Buchanan-Brown)

Basford, Kathleen, 1978, *The green man*

Bettey, J.H., 1979, *Church and community: the parish church in English life*

Bettey, J.H., and Taylor, C.W.G., 1982, *Sacred and satiric:*

medieval stone carving in the west country

Davies, J.G., 1968, *The secular use of church buildings*

Thomas, Keith, 1971, *Religion and the decline of magic*

Amesbury: Chandler, John, and Goodhugh, Peter, 1990, *Amesbury: history and description of a south Wiltshire town*, 2nd ed.

Church Dedications: Everitt, Alan, 1986, *Continuity and colonization: the evolution of Kentish settlement*

Jackson, J.E., 1975, 'Names of Wiltshire churches', *WANHM*, vol.15, 98-110

Crudwell: Vernon, Thelma E., 1962, *Notes on the parish church of All Saints, Crudwell, Wilts.*

Great Bedwyn Guild: Brentnall, H.C., 1948, 'Bedwyn in the tenth century', *WANHM*, vol.52, 360-8

Mere: Baker, T.H., 1907, 'The churchwardens' accounts of Mere', *WANHM*, vol.35, 23-92, 210-82

Pilgrimage: Spencer, Brian, 1990, *Pilgrim souvenirs and secular badges* (Salisbury Museum Medieval Catalogue, pt.2)

Purton: Edwards, John, 1990, 'New light on Christ of the Trades and other medieval wall-paintings at St Mary's, Purton', *WANHM*, vol.83, 105-17

Relics: Timmins, T.C.B., 1984, *The register of John Chandler, Dean of Salisbury 1404-17* (Wiltshire Record Society, vol.39)

Salisbury: Chandler, John, 1983, *Endless Street: a history of Salisbury and its people*

Sheela-na-gigs: Woodcock, Alex, and Oakley, Theresa, 2006, 'The Romanesque corbel-table at St. John's, Devizes, and its Sheela-na-gig', WANHM, vol.99, 250-4

Establishment Figures

General: Chadwick, Owen, 1964, *The Reformation*

Ransome, Mary (ed.), 1972, *Wiltshire returns to the bishop's visitation queries 1783* (Wiltshire Record Society, vol.27)

Spaeth, Donald A., 1988, 'Common prayer? popular observance of the Anglican liturgy in Restoration Wiltshire', in *Parish, church and people: local studies in lay religion 1350-1750*, edited by S.J. Wright

Chilmark: Raikes, Francis, c.1920, *Recollections of village life on Salisbury Plain*

Ferebe: Gandy, Ida, 1989, *Round about the little steeple. . . ,* new ed.

Herbert: Blyth, Ronald, 2005, *George Herbert in Bemerton*

Forrest, Frances, 1955, *George Herbert of Bemerton. . .*

Wall, J.N. jr. (ed.), 1981, *George Herbert: the Country Parson, the Temple*

Mere: Baker -see ch.4

Monuments: Curl, James S., 1980, *A celebration of death*

Sherlock, Peter (ed.), 2000, *Monumental inscriptions of Wiltshire . . .* (Wiltshire Record Society, vol.53)

Parish Administration: Tate, W.E., 1969, *The parish chest: a study of the records of parochial administration*, 3rd ed.

Salisbury: Swayne, H.J.F., 1896, *Churchwardens' accounts of S. Edmund and S. Thomas, Sarum, 1443-1702. . .*

Smith's Diary: Bradby, Edward, 1988, 'The diary of Thomas Smith of Shaw, 1715-23', *WANHM*, vol.82, 115-141

Dissenting Voices

General: Chandler, J.H. (ed.), 1985, *Wiltshire dissenters' meeting house certificates and registrations 1689-1852* (Wiltshire Record Society, vol.40)

Council for British Archaeology, 1985, *Hallelujah! recording chapels and meeting houses*

Davies, Rupert E., 1963, *Methodism*

Reeves, Marjorie E., 1956, 'Protestant nonconformity',

Victoria History of Wiltshire, vol.3, 99-149

Stell, Christopher, 1991, *An inventory of nonconformist chapels and meeting-houses in south-west England* (Royal Commission on the Historical Monuments of England)

Underdown, David, 1985, *Revel, riot, and rebellion: popular politics and culture in England 1603-1660*

Watts, Michael R., 1978, *The Dissenters: from the Reformation to the French Revolution*

Baydon, etc.: Timmins, T.C.B. (ed.), 1984, *The register of John Chandler, Dean of Salisbury 1404-17* (Wiltshire Record Society, vol.39)

Bayntun, Sir Edward: Freeman, Jane, 1988, *The commonplace book of Sir Edward Bayntun of Bromham* (Wiltshire Record Society, vol.43)

Bratton: Reeves, Marjorie, 1978, *Sheep bell and ploughshare: the story of two village families*

Conventicles, 1669: Webb, E. Doran, 1890-3, 'Conventicles in Sarum Diocese, [sc]AD 1669', *Transactions of the Salisbury Field Club*, vol.1, 36-44

Independents: Antrobus, Alfred, 1947, *History of the Wilts. and East Somerset Congregational Union. . .1797-1947*

Jeremy, David J. 1966, 'A local crisis between establishment and nonconformity: the Salisbury village preaching controversy, 1798-1799', *WANHM*, vol.61, 63-84

Quakers: Fassnidge, Harold, 1992, *The Quakers of Melksham 1669-1950*

Primitive Methodism: Tonks, William C., 1907, *Victory in the villages: the history of the Brinkworth circuit*

Religious Census, 1851: Census of Great Britain 1851, 1853, *Religious worship: England and Wales: report and tables*

Salisbury St Thomas's: Hollaender, Albert, 1944, 'The doom painting of St Thomas of Canterbury, Salisbury', *WANHM*, vol.50, 351-70

Southwick: Doel, William, 1890, *Twenty golden candlesticks! or a history of Baptist nonconformity in western Wiltshire*

Wylye: Ingram, Martin, 1987, *Church courts, sex and marriage in England, 1570-1640*

The Victorians and After

General: Clarke, Basil F.L., 1969, *Church builders of the nineteenth century*, revised edition

Cowie, L.W., 1956, 'The Church of England since 1837', *Victoria history of Wiltshire*, vol.3, 57-86

Gilbert, Alan D., 1976, *Religion and society in industrial England*

Howell, Peter, and Sutton, Ian, (ed.) 1989, *The Faber guide to Victorian churches*

also Pevsner and Cherry, 1975; and RCHM, 1987 [see ch.2]

Catholicism: Trappes-Lomax, T.B., 1956, 'Roman Catholicism', *Victoria history of Wiltshire*, vol.3, 87-98

Williams, J.Anthony, 1968, *Catholic recusancy in Wiltshire, 1660-1791*

Cholderton: Gibbon, R.G., 1978, 'Cholderton Church and its builder', *WANHM*, vol.70/71, 104-8

Goddard: Goddard, Francis, 1928, *Reminiscences of a Wiltshire vicar, 1814-1893* [published in weekly instalments in the Wiltshire Gazette, 7th June 1928 - 22nd November 1928; photocopy in Wiltshire Local Studies Library]

Kilvert: Plomer, William (ed.), 1938-40, *Kilvert's diary*, 3 vols.

Price, D.T.W., 1978, 'Francis Kilvert as a clergyman', *A Kilvert symposium*, edited by Frederick Grice, 9-20

Patney: Wiltshire Record Office, WSRO 509/10; 509/11; DI/61/27/12

Wardour: Caraman, Philip, 1984, *Wardour: a short history*

Gazetteer

by Derek Parker

THIS LIST INCLUDES by no means all the Wiltshire churches and chapels worth visiting, but it does offer brief notes on some of those which the authors feel will most interest readers of this book. National grid references are given, and these can be used in conjunction with the map which follows this gazetteer to locate churches. In many cases further information about, and illustrations of, buildings listed here will be found in the main text, via the index. Some churches, and most chapels, are normally kept locked, and so only the exterior may be visible. A few former places of worship are now privately owned. This gazetteer has been greatly expanded from that published in the first edition of this work. To save space centuries have been abbreviated, thus 12C = twelfth century, etc.

Aldbourne: St Michael SU 2675

Fine, interesting Perpendicular church with good Norman arcades, where the original circular arches were rebuilt with

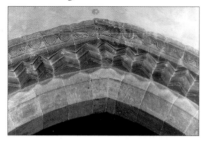

pointed arches. Jacobean pulpit. Two 18C fire engines. Interesting carved stone monuments of 1501.

Alderbury: Ivychurch SU 1827

Remains of an Augustinian monastery now in the structure and garden of a private house.

Alderbury: St Mary SU 1826

Fine 19C church. Built largely of flint. Communion rail contains wrought iron panels.

All Cannings: All Saints SU 0661

Imposing church with a Perp. crossing tower. Much decorated Victorian chancel. Monument to William Ernle has quaint lettering.

Alton Barnes: St Mary SU 1062

Small church with Anglo-Saxon nave (external 'long-and-short' quoins). Three-decker pulpit. Chancel rebuilt 1743.

Alton Priors: All Saints SU 1162

Now redundant. Interesting brass plate to William Button, showing the gates of heaven. Also a yew tree in churchyard said to be 1,700 years old.

Amesbury: St Mary and St Melor SU 1541

Large church associated with Benedictine nunnery, built of flint and basically Norman. 12C font of Purbeck marble. Remains of 9C wheel cross. Beautifully carved 15C and 16C roofs.

Ansty: St James ST 9526

Small 13C and 14C village church. Norman font. Mid-17C carved stalls rescued from Salisbury Cathedral. Lovely village setting with pond, manor farmhouse, and probably the hospice of the preceptory of the Knights Hospitallers nearby.

Ashton Keynes: Holy Cross SU 0494

Moderately large church with Norman chancel arch and arcade. Four preaching crosses at various locations in the churchyard and in the village nearby.

Atworth: St Michael ST 8565

Church built 1832 with separate Perp. tower.

Avebury: St James SU 1069

Medium-size church with Anglo-Saxon windows and Norman arch, arcades and superb font. Fine Perpendicular rood screen. Church situated near the famous prehistoric stone circle.

Bemerton: St Andrew SU 1230

Small 12C—13C church. 17C rector was the poet, George Herbert, who lived in the rectory next door, and is buried in the churchyard.

Biddestone: St Nicholas ST 8673

Bell turret built on ridge of nave. Norman doorway, tympanum, font and two windows.

Bishop's Cannings: St Mary SU 0364

Very fine large church of 12C and 13C, with tall spire. Built by Bishops of Salisbury. Contains a strangely painted penitential seat.

Bishopstone (near Salisbury): St John Baptist SU 0625

A large ornate mostly Dec. church with some Norman work. Impressive interior, a fine tomb chest and a Pugin window.

Bonham: St Benedict ST 7733
Roman Catholic chapel attached to manor house. Now converted into a private residence.

Box: Chapel Plaister ST 8468
Small 15C building, originally a hospice and chapel for pilgrims en route to Glastonbury.

Boyton: St Mary ST 9539
Interesting church entered through an elaborately carved 13C doorway. Late-13C Giffard chapel with a remarkable circular window. Early tombs.

Bradenstoke: Providence Chapel SU 0079
Small chapel dated 1777, with minister's house attached. Remains of Augustinian priory nearby.

Bradford on Avon: St Laurence ST 8260
Small Saxon church, lost for many years and rediscovered in 1856. Probably the finest complete Saxon church in England. Two interesting carved angels set high in the walls. Opposite is **Holy Trinity**, a fine clothiers' Perpendicular church, with earlier features.

Bradford on Avon: St Mary, Tory ST 8261
The chapel of a hospice in a fine position overlooking the town.

Bratton: Baptist Chapel ST 9152
Delightful brick building dated 1734, with attached school rooms and vestry.

Bremhill: Stanley Abbey ST 9672
Large area of disturbed ground and a ruined farmhouse and yard are all that remains of Wiltshire's only Cistercian monastery.

Britford: St Peter SU 1628
Believed to date from 9C. Pre-conquest carving of exceptional interest. Tall narrow nave with windows set high in the walls indicate early date of church.

Bromham: St Nicholas ST 9665
Medium-size village church with spire originally Norman. Ornate Baynton chantry chapel added 1492. Good brass to John Baynton. East window designed by William Morris. Several fine 15C and 16C tombs. Unusual timber lock-up in churchyard.

Broughton Gifford: St Mary ST 8763
Imposing Early English church with entrance porch built into side chapel.

Bulford: St George SU 1843
Army garrison church. Large Perp. style built *1927*.

Bulford: St Leonard SU 1643
Large flint church with squat tower. Traces of wall paintings. Cast iron parish chest.

Burbage: All Saints SU 2361
Exterior of flint and stone built in 1954 and 1876 although the squat tower is old.

Burcombe: St John Baptist SU 0731
Anglo-Saxon with long and short quoins.

Buttermere: St James SU 3461
Small and isolated with 13C windows. Norman font.

Calne: St Mary ST 9971
Large Perpendicular town church built with money from cloth trade. Five-bay Norman arcade largely rebuilt following the collapse of the crossing tower in 1638.

Castle Combe: St Andrew ST 8477
Pleasant village church with very fine carved chancel arch.

14C monument consisting of a tomb chest with effigy of a cross-legged castellan surrounded by mourners.

Castle Eaton: St Mary SU 1595
Situated near River Thames. Norman doorway and font.

Charlton Chapel , Donhead ST 9022
Neo Norman built 1839 but inside has genuine Norman posts supporting a gallery

Charlton Park: St John Baptist ST 9588
Much restored but interesting with Norman font and imposing monument to Sir Henry Knyvett.

Cherhill: St James SU 0370
Small Perp. church with manor house alongside.

Chilton Foliat: St Mary SU 3170
Jacobean nave roof, good screen and interesting monuments. Pearce family mausoleum in churchyard.

Chippenham: St Andrew ST 9173
Spacious town church, largely 19C rebuilding with a fine relocated Norman arch. Ornate south chapel built in 1442 and a fine 1730 organ case. 13C stone carving of a lady with a Norman inscription. Interesting monuments and a fine 13C chest.

Chirton: St John Baptist SU 0757
Fine medium-size village church with much Norman and Decorated work of interest. Particularly good Norman font and 15C stained glass. Wooden nave roof believed to be Norman, c.1200.

Chisbury: Medieval Chapel SU 2766
Ruined chapel of ease built of flint with a thatched roof. Window openings show remains of 13C tracery. Building stands in a farmyard just inside the eastern entrance of Chisbury iron age hillfort.

Chitterne: All Saints ST 9944
Imposing church and tower built 1863 of flint and stone in chequer pattern. Norman font.

Chitterne: St Mary ST 9843
Small chapel being all that remains of original church.

Cholderton: St Nicholas SU 2242
Imposing church built 1840-50. Small turret with bellcote. Medieval hammerbeam roof brought from Ipswich. Mid-19C furnishings and late-12C font.

Chute Forest: St Mary SU 3151
Fine Victorian flint and red brick building with a tall shingled pyramidal spire. Remotely sited away from other buildings, church is in the care of the Redundant Churches Trust.

Clyffe Pypard: St Peter SU 0776
Somewhat over-restored 15C church in beautiful village setting below a wooded hillside. Fine carved pulpit of 1629. A number of interesting monuments, including one to a carpenter, Thomas Spackman, which includes carved tools of his trade. Nikolaus Pevsner and his wife are buried in the churchyard.

Codford: St Mary ST 9739
Good village chequer-pattern church with 14C tower. Norman font. Jacobean pulpit. In neighbouring **St Peter's** very finely carved tapered cross shaft thought to date from 9C.

Colerne: St John Baptist ST 8271
Fine church with Perpendicular tower situated in a magnificent position in this hilltop village. Somewhat over-restored four bay arcades, c.1200-10. Two large fragments of 9C crosses beautifully carved.

Collingbourne Kingston: St Mary SU 2355
Another much restored Norman church. Main item of interest is a huge stone monument to Sir Gabriel Pile and his wife, 1626.

Compton Bassett: St Swithun SU 0372
Quite large church situated on rising ground at one end of the long straggling village. Externally Perpendicular but much Norman work remains inside. Particularly fine 16C stone rood screen. 15C ceiling with carved wooden head bosses.

Corsham: St Bartholomew ST 8770
Important 'wool' church. 15C bench ends and interesting monuments. Corsham Court nearby. In Monks Lane, near Gastard, is quite delightful 17C **Congregational Chapel**

(originally Quaker) with intact interior, gallery on three sides, box pews and pulpit.

Corston: All Saints ST 9283
Unusual stone bell turret on ridge of small brick church.

Cricklade: St Sampson SU 1093
Large church with magnificent 16C tower. Vaulted roof with 64 fine bosses. Ancient cross in churchyard. Nearby, **St**

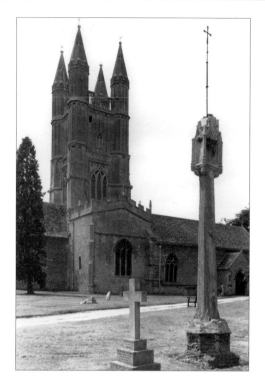

Mary's is a small church (now Catholic), partly Norman. 14C cross in churchyard.

Crudwell: All Saints ST 9592

Contains work of 12-14C, but high narrow shape of nave may indicate the proportions of a Saxon church. Interesting medieval glass and fine carved bench ends.

Dauntsey: St James ST 9782

Interesting church with Norman doorways, box pews and good tomb chest monuments.

Devizes: St James SU 0161

Fine Perp. tower with civil war cannon ball holes in it.

Devizes: St John SU 0061

Large church (originally castle chapel) with Norman tower and chancel. Built by Bishop Roger , it contains some of the finest Norman architecture in the country. Ornate Beauchamp chapel. Nearby is **St Mary,** the original town church, also Norman and contemporary with St John. Only the chancel contains Norman work. Nave and tower are Perpendicular.

Dilton Marsh: Holy Trinity ST 8449

Imposing although built 1844 in 'Norman' style.

Ditteridge: St Christopher ST 8169

Nave and chancel with bellcote on ridge at join. Good Norman doorway, window and font.

Downton: St Lawrence SU 1821

Large church with crossing tower and much of interest to see inside.

Durnford: St Andrew SU 1337

Remarkably spacious Norman church with fine carved work. Perfect example of 12C parish church. Fine Norman font and 15C bench ends and traces of medieval wall paintings.

East Grafton: St Nicholas SU 2560

A fine 'Norman' church with an imposing tower built 1844.

East Knoyle: St Mary ST 8830

Most interesting originally Saxon or Norman village church. Sir Christopher Wren was born here. His father, the rector, was responsible for extensive plasterwork in the chancel, which cost him his living during the commonwealth period.

East Tytherton: Moravian Settlement ST 9674

Brick-built chapel, 1792, in line with the sisters' and minister's houses on either side.

Edington: St Mary, St Katherine and All Saints ST 9253
Very fine cruciform early Perpendicular church set on a fine site overlooking the Vale of Avon and the priory associated

with the church. Especially interesting in that no major restoration or rebuilding has taken place since it was consecrated in 1361. Fabric is in remarkably good order.

Enford: All Saints and St Margaret SU 1351
Quite large and interesting church with impressive Norman arcades and chancel arch. Approached through a short corridor from the chancel is an unusual 13C octagonal vestry.

Etchilhampton: St Andrew SU 0460
Nave and bellcote. Norman font and interesting tomb chest

monument. Several very early grave stones in churchyard.

Farley: All Saints SU 2229
17C brick church with stone dressings, it was built by Sir Stephen Fox, a contemporary of Wren and member of the commission which built Chelsea Hospital. Contemporary furnishings. Interesting brick almshouses opposite the church of similar date.

Fisherton Delamere: St Nicholas SU 0038
Rebuilt 1833, but Norman masonry incorporated into the walls. Interesting monument to two infant children of the rector (Thomas Crockford), who died 1622 and 1624, one child depicted in bed, the other wrapped in a shroud. Church set in fine position overlooking delightful village.

Fovant: St George SU 0028
Contains several reset Norman items. A strange tomb in the churchyard with a steel grid over it.

Great Bedwyn: St Mary SU 2764
Impressive church containing much fine 12C and 13C work, some of which reconstructed. Interesting monuments

including tomb of Sir John Seymour. Almost complete preaching cross in churchyard.

Great Chalfield: All Saints ST 8663
Small stone church closely associated with the adjacent manor house; both are surrounded by a moat. 15C church contains much of interest including a Georgian three-decker pulpit.

Great Wishford: St Giles SU 0735
Village church with tower. Norman font. Jacobean chest. Royal arms carved before 1707. Old fire engine. Interesting monuments. Set in churchyard wall are stones inscribed to record the price of bread at dates since 1800.

Hardenhuish: St Nicholas ST 9074
Small 18C church with a tower having domed octagonal top. Ashlar faced Bath stone throughout, and designed by John Wood of Bath.

Heytesbury: St Peter and St Paul ST 9242
Large 13C church but much restored. Fine 16C stone

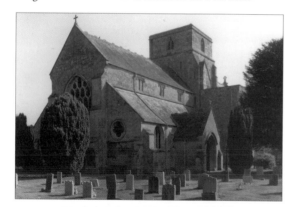

screen. The pillars of the choir arcade are embellished with Purbeck marble shafts in the style of Salisbury Cathedral.

Horningsham: Meeting House ST 8141
Claims to be the oldest nonconformist chapel in the country, with datestone 1566. Present building, c.1700, is excellent example of early chapel interior.

Horningsham: St John Baptist ST 8241
Has fine Perp. tower. Church set in good position overlooking valley.

Hullavington: St Mary ST 8982
Largely 13C with Somerset style Perp. tower rebuilt 1880. Nice 17C carved wood panel.

Imber: St Giles ST 9648
Externally Perp. but contains 13C arcades. Situated within MOD battle area and rarely open to the public.

Inglesham: St John Baptist SU 2098

Small, charming unrestored rustic church, largely 13C.

Elizabethan pulpit. Good box pews. Interesting Saxon sculpture of Virgin and Child beneath the hand of God.

Keevil: St Leonard ST 9258

Good village church, largely late Perpendicular. Very early bell.

Kellaways: St Giles ST 9475

Small 18C chapel built alongside Maud Heath's Causeway.

Kingston Deverill: St Mary ST 8437

1846 nave and south aisle also a 15C central tower. Fine massive timber roof structure.

Knook: St Margaret ST 9341

Small Norman church close to manor house. Very fine carved tympanum of a style reminiscent of illuminated manuscripts.

Lacock: St Cyriac ST 9168

Impressive Perpendicular church. Several fine monuments, particularly that to Sir William Sharington, 1566. Nearby is Lacock Abbey, now mansion. Originally built 1229 for Augustinian canonesses. Cloisters and conventual buildings remain as nucleus of house built 1540. In 19C the home of W.H. Fox Talbot, pioneer of photography.

Larkhill: St Alban SU 1244

Red brick garrison church built 1937.

Latton: St John Baptist SU 0995

Perpendicular village church with considerable Norman remains. Two fragments of Roman columns in the nave.

Leigh Delamere: St Margaret ST 8879

Interesting stone sanctus bell turret. Built 1846.

Limpley Stoke: St Mary ST 7860

Small unrestored church in a beautiful situation. Notable 10C or 11C doorway built into the south arcade.

Little Langford: St Nicholas SU 0436

Small country church with well carved Norman south doorway and tympanum.

Littlecote: Roman Villa SU 2970

In grounds of Littlecote House. Very fine mosaic pavement showing Apollo playing a harp, with possible Christian connotations.

Ludgershall: St James SU 2650
Large flint and rubble church with important imposing monument to Sir Richard Brydges, 1558.

Lydiard Tregoze: St Mary SU 1084
Medium-size 15C church close to Lydiard Park mansion. Contains numerous 16C and 17C monuments with original railings and several helms. Considerable remains of wall painting.

Malmesbury: Abbey Church ST 9387
Founded 7C, and rebuilt in several stages into a huge structure of which only a section remains of high-standard largely Norman work. South porch has Norman carving considered to be amongst the finest in England, although now badly weathered. Interesting museum. Nearby, in Bristol Street, Westport, is a recently-discovered **Saxon Chapel**, now an occupied cottage. 'Long-and-short quoins' clearly visible.

Manningford Bruce: St Peter SU 1457
A complete Norman church sensitively restored in 1882. A real gem.

Marden: All Saints SU 0857
Pleasant village church with fine Norman south doorway. Jacobean pulpit. Impressive modern glass.

Market Lavington: St Mary SU 1054
13C stone church with many pieces of carved Norman masonry incorporated into the structure. Saxon cemetery nearby, recently excavated.

Marlborough College Chapel SU 1868
Built 1877 to a design by Burne Jones.

Marlborough: St Mary SU 1869
Substantial church rebuilt in 1653 after mainly Norman original was burnt down in a great fire, which also destroyed much of the town. Fire damage still visible on Norman column. Vandalized Roman stone carving depicting *Fortuna*, later identified with St Katherine.

Melksham: Nonconformist Chapels ST 9063
Several good chapels: **Quaker Meeting House** (now Spiritualist Church) of 1734; **Baptist Chapel** of 1776; **Methodist Chapel**, 1872, somewhat highly ornamented.

Melksham: St Michael ST 9063
Large Perp. church with traces of its Norman predecessor. Many interesting tablet memorials.

Mere: St Michael ST 8132
Fine Perpendicular structure with a lofty tower and good screens. An example of 14C-15C High Gothic at its best. Very fine Bettesthorne chantry chapel. Well carved 15C misericords.

Mildenhall: St John Baptist SU 2169
Perfect example of a small village church of many periods,

from Anglo-Saxon onwards. Late Georgian 'Gothick' fittings throughout, recently beautifully refurbished.

Milton Lilbourne: St Peter SU 1860
Early English with a fine window engraving by Whistler.

Monkton Farleigh: St Peter ST 8065
Rebuilt 1844 but retains a Norman doorway and 13C tower.

Netheravon: All Saints SU 1448
11C tower and 12C nave. Anglo-Saxon porticus.

Netherhampton: St Catherine SU 1029
Built 1876 in stone but has an 18C tower built in brick and topped with an unusual timber 'house'.

North Newnton: St James SU 1357
Massive timber beams supporting the bell frames protrude beyond the faces of the tower and are protected from the weather by separate small stone roofs.

Norton: All Saints ST 8884
Small church with an oversize and ornamental bell turret.

Oaksey: All Saints ST 9993
Interesting Norman and 13C church. 15C wall paintings and stained glass. Stone 'sheela-na-gig' set in the north wall.

Oare: Holy Trinity SU 1563
Built 1858 in brick in neo-Norman style.

Ogbourne St Andrew: St Andrew SU 1872
Medium-size village church with Norman elements remaining. A large tree-covered bowl barrow in the churchyard.

Old Dilton: St Mary ST 8649
Delightful small Perpendicular chapel of ease with a bell

turret and spire. Unspoilt 18C furnishings including three-decker pulpit, box and family pews and two separate galleries.

Pewsey: St John Baptist SU 1659
A mixed bag of Norman, 13C and 14C. Interesting tall carved wooden font cover.

Potterne: St Mary ST 9958
Very fine Early English church, little altered structurally. An Anglo-Saxon font with a Latin inscription on the rim is in the church, but probably came originally from a wooden Saxon baptistery excavated nearby.

Preshute: St George SU 1868
Largely 19C externally, but contains 12C four-bay arcade. C13 black Tournai marble font believed to have come from Marlborough Castle.

Purton: St Mary SU 0887
Interesting church close to manor house. Unusual in having

both tower and spire. Large wall paintings in reasonable condition.

Ramsbury: Holy Cross SU 2771
Fine church containing many interesting furnishings including finely-carved remnants of 9C crosses and several

fine monuments. Church built on early minster site, which was bishop's seat in 10C-11C.

Rodbourne: Holy Rood ST 9383
Some Norman work and an unusual tower. Inside there is a circular chair carved from solid stone, thought to be 13C.

Salisbury SU 1429
Cathedral commenced 1220. Apart from the later spire (the loftiest in England) the structure is almost all in Early English style. Contains many monuments of great interest. Chapter House, with carved frieze of Old Testament scenes, contains a remarkable collection of church plate and a copy of Magna Carta. Fine cloisters. Beautiful setting surrounded by close of fine buildings, including medieval deanery and canons' houses. St Francis is a red brick 'Odeon' style suburban church, built 1939. **St Martin** predates establishment of the city. Contains a fine example of a 15C brass eagle lectern. St Osmund, the Catholic church, was designed by Pugin. **St Thomas** is a good Perpendicular city centre church, with noteworthy late-medieval Doom painting over the chancel arch, and superb roof timbering.

Sandy Lane: St Nicholas ST 9668

A cosy wooden church, built 1892, with thatched roof and wooden font.

Savernake Forest: St Katharine SU 2565
Good example of a Victorian church built in 13C style for the Tottenham Park estate.

Seend: Holy Cross ST 9460
Largely Perp. and built with 'cloth' money. There is a cloth-trimming shears carved in stone in the surround of one of the West windows.

Shaw: Christ Church ST 8966
Interesting Arts and Crafts Movement church, built 1905. Masonry exterior with good carved figures on the tower. Interior all timber.

Sherston: Holy Cross ST 8586
Fine large church with lofty Gothic-style tower, built in fact in 1730. Late four-bay Norman arcade. Interesting monuments. Famous stone figure known as 'Rattlebone'.

South Wraxall: St James ST 8364
Picturesque tower dated 1300.

South Wraxall: Manor Farmhouse ST 8364
(North of the Manor House) Originally 14C hospice, chapel and hall. Several windows and doorway remain from 14C, with 17C extensions.

Southwick Baptist Chapel ST 8355
Square brick building with an open air baptistery by a nearby stream.

Southwick: St Thomas ST 8355
Completed 1904. Unusually for an Anglican building it contains a baptistery for total immersion. Baptist Chapel is a large brick building of 1815. Open air baptistery nearby, associated with a stream.

Stanton Fitzwarren: St Leonard SU 1790
Interesting village church with superb carved Norman font and much well-carved woodwork.

Stanton St Bernard: All Saints SU 0962
19C rebuilt church, with Norman font. Strange Edwardian painting over chancel arch.

Stanton St Quintin: St Giles ST 9079
Fine church with Norman tower and unusual Norman carving on capitals, doorway, and figure of Christ standing on a dragon.

Stapleford: St Mary SU 0737
Very fine Norman arcade of four bays and south doorway. Situated above a pretty village.

Steeple Ashton: St Mary ST 9056
Magnificent 'clothiers' church with a tower which was surmounted by a steeple until blown down in 1670. Original stone vaulting to nave then replaced by wooden imitation. Superb stone lierne vaulting in aisles, chapels and chancel.

Stockton: St John Baptist ST 9838
Norman arcade and font. Fine wooden screen and good monuments.

Stratford sub Castle: St Lawrence SU 1332
Small village church well situated by River Avon immediately below Old Sarum. 13C chancel and tower rebuilt 1711. Date and benefactor's name inscribed in large letters on tower exterior.

Sutton Veny: St John Evangelist ST 9041
Impressive Victorian church with spire (1868).

Swindon SU 1584
Christ Church is large church, 1851 by Sir Gilbert Scott, with tower and broach spire. **St Aldhelm** is a small, simple town centre church, built 1968. **St Mark**, near the former railway works, was built 1845 to serve New Swindon. **St Paul**, Covingham was built 1971 as church centre and library to serve new housing estate.

Teffont Evias: St Michael and All Angels ST 9932
Built 1826 with tall steeple. Nicely situated close to manor house. Several good monuments.

Tidcombe: St Michael SU 2958
Flint and rubble construction. A delightful small unimproved country church in an attractive village.

Tilshead: St Thomas of Canterbury SU 0347
Large church of flint and stone, partly in chequer pattern. Low central tower. Three-bay Norman arcade of exceptionally simple design. Norman font. Church disproportionately large for present village, which was Domesday borough.

Tisbury: Place Barn ST 9529
Largest tithe barn in England. 15C stone under thatch. Built for Shaftesbury Abbey.

Tisbury: St John ST 9429
Large church with a crossing tower largely rebuilt in 1762. Much 12C, 13C and 14C work visible. Mausoleum to the Arundell family beneath the chancel.

Tockenham: St Giles SU 0379
Small church noteworthy for shingled spire supported by wooden posts. Roman altar set in exterior south wall.

Trowbridge ST 8557
Holy Trinity. Early Victorian church (1838). Large with

massive tower and ugly interior. **St James.** Large medieval church, much restored, with spire. Interesting stained glass and Norman coffin lids. **Tabernacle Church.** Impressive Victorian Congregational chapel with tower, and magnificent interior with large organ and balconies. Large Sunday school attached. Several other chapels in this nonconformist town.

Tytherington: St James ST 9141
Small medieval church.

Upavon: St Mary SU 1355
Large Norman church, much restored. Massive 13C tower and arcades. Norman font.

Urchfont: St Michael SU 0457
Long, low, impressive church notable for its 14C lierne-vaulted chancel. Interesting monuments. 13C font.

Wardour: Chapel ST 9327
Built 1776 as the private Catholic chapel of New Wardour Castle. Magnificent interior with remarkably opulent furnishings ablaze with paint and gold leaf. Large oil paintings.

West Dean: Borbach Chantry SU 2527
Now used as a mortuary chapel. It is all that remains of St. Mary's church. Contains several fine monuments.

West Lavington: All Saints SU 0053
Substantial village church with 12C four-bay arcade. Many fine monuments.

Westbury: All Saints ST 8751
Large much renewed Perp. church with interesting monuments and beautifully carved wooden pulpit. Several large nonconformist chapels.

Westwood: St Mary ST 8159
Fine ashlar-faced church with imposing Perpendicular tower in Somerset style. Some 12C and 13C items. Westwood Manor is alongside.

Whaddon: St Mary ST 8861
Small, isolated and unused but has a fine Norman tympanum over the south door.

Wilsford-cum-Lake: St Michael SU 1339
Norman tower with herringbone pattern flintwork. Monuments include one by Eric Gill.

Wilton: St Mary and St Nicholas SU 0931
Built 1845 for the Herbert family in Italian Romanesque style. Tall detached campanile. Amazing collection of furnishings and stained glass in the impressive interior.

Winterbourne Gunner: St Mary SU 1835
Small simple church with Norman flint and rubble tower now plastered and painted.

Winterbourne Monkton: St Mary Magdalene SU 0971
Rebuilt 1878 but retains many features of the earlier structures. A good Norman font.

Wootton Rivers: St Andrew SU 1962
Built of flint with a wooden bell turret topped by a shingled spire. One of the faces of the turret clock has the words 'GLORYBETOGOD' instead of numbers 1 to 12.

| 70 | 80 | 90 | 00 | 10 | 20 | 30 | 00 |

Inglesham
Latton
Castle Eaton
Crudwell Oaksey Ashton Cricklade Highworth
Keynes
Stanton Fitzwarren

90 Charlton Park Minety **90**

Purton Stratton St Margaret
MALMESBURY Lydiard Tregoze
Sherston Bremilham SWINDON
Luckington Rodbourne Brinkworth
Norton Wootton Wanborough
Alderton Corston Dauntsey Bassett
Hullavington Wroughton
80 Grittleton Stanton St Quintin Tockenham **80**
Sutton Benger Christian
Leigh Delamere Kington Malford Clyffe
W Kington Castle St Michael Bradenstoke Pyppard Broad Hinton Chiseldon
Combe Kellaways E Tytherton Hilmarton Winterbourne Bassett Aldbourne
Hardenhuish CHIPPENHAM Charlcote Ogbourne St George
Slaughterford Biddestane Bremhill Winterbourne Monkton Ogbourne St Andrew
Colerne Derry Hill Stanley Compton Bassett Temple Ramsbury Littlecote
70 Corsham CALNE Avebury Rockley Mildenhall Chilton **70**
Ditteridge Box Lacock Sandy Lane Cherhill Clatford Froxfield Foliat
Preshute MARLBOROUGH
Atworth Shaw Bromham Stanton Cadley Chisbury
Monkton Farleigh St Bernard Savernake Forest
S Wraxall MELKSHAM Bishops Cannings Oare Great Bedwyn
Limpley Gt Chalfield Broughton Gifford Allington Alton Wootton Rivers
60 Stoke Whaddon Seend All Cannings Priors Burbage Buttermere **60**
Keevil DEVIZES Alton Barnes Pewsey Easton Grafton
BRADFORD ON AVON Patney N Newnton Milton Tidcombe
TROWBRIDGE Steeple Potterne Chirton Manningford Collingbourne
Southwick Ashton Urchfont Marden Bruce Kingston
North Bradley Upavon Chute
Brokerswood Heywood Edington Market Lavington Enford
50 WESTBURY Bratton West Lavington **50**
Dilton Marsh Old Dilton Imber Tilshead Netheravon Ludgershall
WARMINSTER Boreham Orcheston Larkhill Durrington
Bishopstrow Chitterne Maddington Bulford Cholderton
Longleat Heytesbury Knook Rollestone
Horningsham Sutton Veny Codford Berwick Amesbury
40 Tytherington Boyton Fisherton St James Wilsford **40**
Maiden Bradley Sherrington Wylye Durnford
Kingston Steeple Langford Stapleford
Deverill Little Langford Woodford Winterbourne Dauntsey
Stourton Great Wishford Stratford Winterbourne Gunner
Bonham Mere W Knoyle Chilmark S Newton sub Castle
Burcombe Wilton Old Sarum
30 E Knoyle Tisbury Teffont Bemerton SALISBURY **30**
Sedgehill Evias Britford Ivychurch Farley
Fovant Netherhampton West Dean
Wardour Bishopstone Odstock Alderbury
Ansty Fifield Standlynch Whiteparish
Bavant Broad Chalke Morgans Vale
Ferne Landford
20 Charlton Downton Redlynch **20**

scale of 10 kilometres

| 70 | 80 | 90 | 00 | 10 | 20 | 30 | |

Index

T HIS IS AN INDEX of places, persons and selected subjects. Some minor references are omitted. Places, other than large towns, are in Wiltshire unless otherwise stated.

Baydon 63, 127
Baynton 35
Bayntun, Edw (Sir) 131
Beauchamp, Eliz 84
Bedwyn *see* Great Bedwyn
bells 102, 104
Bemerton 115, 186
Berwick St James 105
Berwyk, Hen 44-5
bishops 2, 54-8; see *also* Salisbury
Bishop's Cannings 38-40, 63, 100, 114,
    116-17, 186
Bishopstone (north Wilts) 63
Bishopstone (south Wilts) 27, 45, 87,
    186
Bishopstrow 8-9, 14
Bonham 153, 155, 187
Boreham 166
Box 9, 12, 14, 128-9, 187
Boyton 84, 187
Bradenstoke 64-5, 69, 73, 140-1, 187
Bradford-on-Avon 5, 14, 16-17, 27, 28,
    43, 67, 78-81, 83, 90, 92, 93, 131,
    137, 139, 161, 187
Bramshaw (Hants) 118
Bratton 27, 43, 88, 135, 141, 161, 187
Breamore (Hants) 79
Bremhill 187
Bremilham 14, 19
Brinkworth 26, 100, 145-6
Britford 17, 89, 118, 187
Britton, Jn 158
Broad Chalke 64, 104, 145
Broad Hinton 105
Brokerswood 166, 168
Bromham 83-4, 131, 170, 187
Broughton Gifford 27, 129, 154, 187
Bruce, Lord 162

Brunsdon, Symon 104
Buckler, Jn 47-9
Bulford 44, 67, 118, 173, 188
Burbage 35, 64, 127, 188
Burcombe 20, 188
Buttermere 32-4, 188
Button, Wm 124, 186

Cadley (Savernake) 166
Calne 16, 43, 61, 64, 65, 100, 131,
    133, 188
Calstone 61
Calvinism 113, 119, 138
canons 54-5, 63-4
Capon, Jn (Bishop) 109
Castle Combe 2, 43, 61, 62,188
Castle Eaton 188
Cennick, Jn 137-9
Chandler, Jn (Dean) 47
chantries 82-7, 111
Chapel Plaister 187
chapels-of-ease 25-8, 35
Chapmanslade 27, 140
Chardstock (Dorset) 61
Charlcote 131
Charlton, Donhead 188
Charlton Park 188
Chedworth (Glos) 10
Cherhill 9, 61, 188
chests, parish 118
Chilmark 112-13
Chilton Foliat 132, 188
Chippenham 62, 125, 133, 145, 188
Chirton 68-9, 188
Chisbury 21, 35, 188
Chiseldon 35
Chitterne 49, 65, 188
Cholderton 164-5, 189

Christian Malford 19, 145
Christopher (St) 10, 102-3
church houses 90
Chute 166
Chute Forest 166, 189
Cirencester (Glos) 2, 10, 52
Clatford 52
cloth, clothiers 40-3, 46
Clyffe Pypard 125, 149-50, 189
Codford 19, 189
Colerne 19, 92, 132, 189
Collingbourne Kingston 108-9, 125,
    189
Compton, Enford 27
Compton Bassett 30-3, 92, 100, 189
Congregationalists *see* Independents
conventicles 131-3
Coombe, Enford 27
Coople 35
Corsham 105, 127, 133-4, 139, 189
Corsley 28
Corston 189
Covingham 174
Cowage 14, 19
Cricklade 9, 20-1, 46, 62, 100, 146,
    189
Crockford, Thos 114-15
Croucheston 19
Crudwell 13, 88, 190
Cumberwell 14, 133
Cutteridge 133

dancing 89-90
Dauntsey 25-7, 190
dedications, church 89
Derry Hill 144
Devizes 36-8, 44, 47, 56, 85-6, 91,
    104-5, 107, 133, 136, 137, 140,

W HEREVER WE TURN, in town or village, we encounter churches and other Christian buildings — so much so that we tend to take them for granted. If we do venture inside the door, the leaflets on offer rarely take us further than the architectural details. So we miss the great tapestry of social history, geography, folklore, archaeology, art and popular culture which is woven into their fabric.

With its lively and stimulating text and superb photographs this book is intended as an introduction to the fascinating story behind Wiltshire's rich legacy of churches, and as a showpiece for the remarkable architectural and artistic heritage that they embrace. When first published (under a slightly different title) in 1993 this book was warmly received, and it has now been completely redesigned, with revised text and many new images.

From Salisbury Cathedral to the humblest wayside chapel, Wiltshire's places of worship bear witness to a long and often surprising history. This book provides the ideal companion.

ISBN 0-946418-46-2

Hobnob Press

9 780946 418466